The Words We Left Unsaid

a memoir

LAURA
GEORGAKAKOS

CLUSTER PRESS

2014

LIBRARY OF CONGRESS
CONTROL NUMBER:

2012902800

FIFTH PRINTING 2015

ClusterPress@gmail.com

Book design by Barbara M. Bachman

With thanks to God
for the lives of my beloved parents,
Nöel and Gil
and my brothers,
Jess and Nick

For Toby ~
my brother who was there,
my friend who is here.

◦◦◦

For my Kos ~
tender is the knight,
my companion in the light

◦◦◦

For our son ~
honest to Pete
and
for Pete's sake

CONTENTS

Let us lift our hands,
let us touch these faces and please,
let us begin to sing.

— TOBY GORDON

The House on Doe Hill

I.

WE HAVE ALWAYS CALLED IT THE HOUSE WE GREW UP in. It has been nearly forty-five years since we left Doe Hill, and yet when I was in the area recently the first thing I did was to drive out that way. The family existed briefly and only there, and for that reason the house has always been something of a shrine to my brothers and me. In adolescence it was the site to which we made our pained pilgrimage whenever we needed the relief of something solid and unchanged. I didn't know for years that the boys went too. Each of us went alone and secretly. We went there because she had been there, our mother. She had stood on that porch, we remembered her at that window. We went to be where she had been, where we all had been together.

It bothered me as a child that our house had no number—none of the houses on that road did. Everyone who mattered knew who was where, and our mailman knew, and that presumably was enough. But it was not enough for me. I wanted a house number to memorize as my class-mates did. I wanted to know and to be able to write down the exact coordinates of home.

For years it remained home to me in a way no other house ever had been or could be. It was for sale recently, and when I saw its photo in the *New York Times Magazine* I knew it instantly, a thousand miles and decades away though I was. I wondered who was leaving it and why, and I wondered whether they will carry it with them as I and my brothers do. I wonder how many we number, those of us who carry it with us, how large is this oddly conjoined fellowship? As adults my brothers and I make reference to it, when we do, in a slightly embarrassed way as if we can hardly believe the lingering potency of it.

In the same self-conscious way we sometimes try to talk about our mother. But the very first obstacle is what to call her, a matter that too often defeats us before we venture very far into conversation. When we knew her we were very small, and she was Mommy, but as adults that sounds silly and undignified. So we smile sheepish smiles and grow silent.

Her name was Nöel. From a lifetime of studying her photograph I know her face better than I know my own. But she is so long gone that I strain to remember the feel of her hand or the sound of her voice. I take delight in the idea that there was such a time and person—that a woman once lived to whom I was attached by all the ties that connect a mother and child. After she died I sometimes said *Mommy* aloud when I was alone. My mouth missed the word and liked to form it—I had never had the chance to use it up. I would like to have grown old enough with her to try *Mother.* I like the sound of that. Its formality would have been softened by years of *Mommy.* But years of Mommy none of us had.

II.

THE HOUSE HAS NEVER BEEN ONE YOU COULD APPROACH recklessly or quickly, the road cut through woods is too winding. The necessarily slow approach allows a good look at the house and yard. A picket fence runs along the front of the property, the first thing you see as you approach and last thing as you leave. The fence has listed for as long as I can remember. Its pickets point not skyward and sure but rather lean backward, sideways, only vaguely indicating some direction. It fails as a fence but charms as decoration. This unsteady line, wobbly and loose, encircles my childhood home—a white picket fence perhaps mindful of its potency as a symbol and careful not to make any false promises.

A brick pathway leads from the front gate straight up the lawn to the porch. The house is typical of the area—a white dutch colonial with gray-blue shutters and porch. Graceful white pillars run down the length of the front porch. The brick walkway continues around the house on the right and ends at the stone steps to the upper yard and pool. Dad taught the boys and me to swim here almost fifty years ago. The last time I stole across the property and climbed the stone steps I found that the pool—still enclosed by our familiar old chain link fence and gate—is drained and has long been unused. The enclosure now is dense with greenery. Long ago, bushes and trees pushed up through the fractured concrete of the pool and have grown to maturity. You have to look carefully to discern the remains of what was once a very different scene.

The house itself is best dressed in the colors of autumn, best framed by maple and oak and poplar branches bright with leaves. It was still legal to burn in those days, and more than anything now the smell of burning leaves evokes that house and those days when Indian corn hung on our front door and curling colored leaves slid across the porch past toys and trikes and four pumpkins by the door, one for each of us.

Autumn. We children are wearing sweaters and corduroys and laced red leather oxfords in those last days of being able to run from here to there without the snow pants and boots that will soon slow us down. The air is bracing, we move quickly, I feel sharp and alive. Mommy is out there with us, lengths of ivy in her hand from the patch near the front gate. I have seen this scene in a home movie. Winding each strand into a wreath, she plops one on each of our heads as we fall, panting, beside her on the lawn Jess and Nick, me and Toby.

When Jess was born, the doctor said no more children. One was as many as Mommy could handle. But quick as a blink there were four of us under the age of six, and this large house to fit us in, and Dad at work later and later each evening to pay for it and to have some quiet.

Our home movies, like so many of my memories, are true in color but silent. In this autumn scene with its flaming red and orange and yellow leaves overhead, the four of us children are tussling with one another on the lawn and seem all to be talking at once. Someone is filming, so Dad is there. Mommy lifts her head to blow cigarette smoke into the air above us. She is laughing as we talk, reaching to pick a leaf off my sweater, a fleck of tobacco off her tongue. She is at our center and she is lovely and lively. We have her surrounded and she has us enthralled in those last days of being able to run from here to there with nothing to slow us down.

III.

THE STONE THAT MARKS MY MOTHER'S GRAVE HAS THE same pink granite base as all the others in the family plot, but the center of her stone has been cut away to hold a sculpture depicting four young faces. They are our faces, the faces of her children. There we are at seven and nine and ten and twelve years old, locked into that stone, trapped at her grave, bound forever to the place where she is buried. That's how it felt for a long time. Growing up, that's how her suicide felt to me.

Even so, for years I only half-heartedly nibbled at those ties. Part of me wanted to stay close, to be where she was. It seemed disloyal to be alive and happy. For a long time after she died the very ground we children stood upon threatened to give way, to crumble toward her grave as if to enlarge the hole to make room enough for all of us.

That is the way with suicide—it is punishment but also promise. It is death but also dare. It taunts, it whispers your name. A way is opened up, a thought planted, there is suggestion of reunion. There is the example of the beloved, a life choice enacted before your very eyes. One of the many paths open before you has been trod by someone you love and for whom you long. There is a figure ahead and fading fast. Is she beckoning? Shall I follow?

I started to. I wanted to. And following her into suicide was not the only snare. There was also the temptation of living a half-life in her honor, of passively renouncing life out of loyalty to her. This is a slow disappearing act best performed in solitude on an unlit stage. How simple it can be to vacate your life. How easy to let one thing go, and then another, and then another, until you're not really living anymore. Or rather you are living, you just aren't living your own life—you're living hers.

Worse were the counterblows I sent out to punish a world empty of her, devoid of her comfort, her voice. I visited my pain upon Dad for years. In her absence he stood accused of a crime I long refused to forgive: he was not her. Whoever he was, whoever he always had been, whatever he strove so earnestly to provide an aching heart, I deemed it insufficient. I denied him satisfaction. I refused to be comforted.

For too long I insisted that it was Mommy or nothing, and so it was nothing. For a thousand nights and more I curled up to inhabit a dim place darkened by guilt and despair and a willful insistence on reunion with my mother at any cost. My twilight years are not before me but behind. I passed through them early in life.

My exile, a self-imposed one, is over. And the hand too ready to point an accusing finger has been lowered and relaxed. I try not to clutch after that which is gone. I want my hands open and soft to receive what is being delivered.

It requires both hands to take up a weighty childhood. And I take up mine now to set it down on the page. I take up my pen to lay down my past. I let go what was to take up what is, and to raise high real hope of what is to come.

IV.

Mommy at the piano, and we had music in that house. So many of our childhood days were lived out to the accompaniment of Schumann or Rachmaninov. Even more often she sang. She had studied music and voice. She had trained for this, for us, to sing to her children, to teach us to sing. She led us in folksongs and rounds pointing to each of us in turn when it was time to jump in. Jess began us of course, setting our pitch and pace. This was a group effort, a family song. But with each of us alone on our line we young ones sang scared, eager to keep up and to get our part just right.

On weekend afternoons Dad sang barbershop in the living room with his doctor friends. He found his peace in the precision and control of tight four-part harmony. Holding a long note his eyes would close and his eyebrows rise up and his head would shake. *Myyyy Gaaal Saaaal.* We kids giggled at the sight even as we delighted in the sound.

Early on, Dad and Mommy sang together breaking into spontaneous duets at times—a Shaker hymn or Gilbert and Sullivan or show tunes. How rich we children were. Our exposure to music was as wide ranging as their record collection—the big bands and Mozart, Woody Guthrie, Gershwin, Joan Sutherland.

Perhaps only humor shared as exalted a spot in Dad's life as music did. He listened with a grin to Bob & Ray and Nichols & May and Tom Lehrer and Bob Newhart. We rarely understood what was so funny, but who cared when it brought on that knee-slapping, snorting laughter of his. We competed to be his best straight man obediently feeding back the lines he had taught us. He was full of stories and jokes and puns and long before we were old enough to understand, we knew them by heart. With everything else that filled our hearts in those days we made room for the wit and one-liners, the mimicry and laughter that were Dad.

He liked to record all of us singing together and would lug in the heavy reel-to-reel tape recorder from his study and position it in our midst. Setting it up and threading the tape was always a challenge—Dad was all thumbs with machines. But he persisted and insisted and I'm grateful that he did, and for the record we have of the singing at Doe Hill.

As we sang Dad would challenge us to leave the safety of the melody and to venture higher, to seek out that strand of harmony floating just above. Jess was always first to take off after it. He was fearless when it came to music, at perfect ease, in perfect pitch.

When things started to go wrong, when Dad was gone more and more, you would find us some evenings on the living room floor listening to Pete Seeger records with Mommy. She would stretch out, worn out, and we would crawl over her like puppies, stopping here or there to snuggle or to ask a question. Her body was an extension of our own and we roamed her surfaces possessively. How we must have drained her with our need always to be talking, to be touching her. But she lay quietly, abiding us without complaint.

Five o'clock, six o'clock, four wound-up children winding down. Seven o'clock, eight o'clock, in search of comfort we look to her and she looks to the liquor cabinet across the room.

Out the front window day becomes night, and darkness appears, and Dad does not.

V.

OFTEN HE WAS WORKING, MAKING HOUSE CALLS, MAKING rounds, avoiding the pain and frustrations at home. The hospital was familiar, the routine predictable, the crises that came up were ones he was trained to handle. I have a photo of Dad opening the white door of the hospital, a smile on his face, about to duck into the maze of hallways that he knew by heart, about to be lost to whoever snapped the picture, and looking glad of it.

Sometimes on Sunday afternoons he took one or two of us with him on rounds, and it was on those trips that I came to understand the attraction of the hospital. I would have chosen it over home too, had I been offered a choice. It was clean there and orderly. Intriguing thought that I had been born here, that this had been my very first home, this peace and spotlessness, these hushed tones.

At the hospital Dad would park me in the coffee shop and leave me to twirl on my stool at the counter or to peruse the gift shop while he checked on his patients. Afterward he retrieved me with a squeeze to my shoulder. He had good doctor hands, warm and clean. He wore no rings, only a wristwatch, one we would lay an ear against when his hand was close by. It didn't tick-tock like other watches, his hummed. We were intrigued that it could look so like other wristwatches but make so unexpected a sound.

Like his watch, Dad hummed too sometimes. Whenever there was something he was pretending not to notice he would reach for his pipe and start to hum. He would park the stem in clenched teeth as he reached into his suit pocket for his bag of tobacco. Stethoscope always in the right pocket, tobacco in the left. Whenever Dad reached for his pipe and started to hum I would look around in quick survey of the chaos and try to guess what it was in the current mess that he was trying so loudly not to see. It was usually obvious. It was usually Mommy.

Sad, lonesome, exhausted, she slept. As she cooked less and cleaned up less the chaos intensified as did Dad's sense of helplessness and he worked even more. It seemed at times as if he appeared just long enough to shake his head before disappearing again from sight and sound.

More and more when he was home the voices from their bedroom were raised and angry ones as they had their fights. He would emerge afterward and we children would hesitate, shaken by the yelling and unsure which of them to move toward. But if he was the one within reach we would move in his direction—to his smoky pipe smell, to his lap, to his jokes, the funny faces, to the old radio ads he sang. *Use Ajax, Bom bom! The foaming cleanser, bom bombom bom bombom . . .*

He would wrinkle up his forehead at my request and I would rub my fingers across the rounded ridges. I loved the tallness of him. His very size imparted a sense of security. I seemed to be forever looking up into his nose or down at his departing wing tip shoes.

When Mommy would come out of their room, dabbing an eye or belting her robe, feigning indifference to the choice we had made, guilt would seize us—her troops—caught once more fraternizing with the enemy.

VI.

It had all begun so prettily and with such promise. Mommy was the eldest of three daughters of a Texas rancher, a member of one of the founding families of San Antonio—the Mavericks, a family notorious in Texas for over a century for its politics, artistic talents and eccentricities. Cousins are quick to point out that the family has contributed at least two useful words to the English language—*maverick* and *gobbledygook*. Grandpa's great-grandpa, Samuel Maverick, didn't brand his cattle, so all those that stood out from the herd in that way came to be known as Maverick's, later *mavericks*. It is a word that has taken on a life of its own. *Gobbledygook* was coined by Grandpa's uncle Maury Maverick to describe the wordy, unintelligible nonsense that flew back and forth in Congress during his tenure as Democratic congressman under FDR and mentor to Lyndon Johnson.

My mother grew up surrounded by scores of relatives

on the Maverick family's Sunshine Ranch in San Antonio. The ranch spread out over a large area and included a certified dairy farm, a tackle shop, cattle, corn and bean fields, fig and peach and pecan trees, dogs and peacocks, turkeys, pigs and guineas, and thirty houses and barns and cabins most of which were filled to the rafters with aunts and uncles and greats and great-greats. There were cousins of every age to play or fight with or to be teased by. There were horses to ride and the creek to wade in, quilting bees, baseball games in the evenings and sleepovers among the kids.

For over forty years a Sunday night potluck supper was held up the road at the Big House where Mommy's great-grandparents, Jane and Albert Maverick, had raised their eleven children and lived together as man and wife for seventy years. They gave each of their children some of the land, which the children, when grown, then subdivided among their own children. The result was a country commune that survived for decades through the Depression and two world wars.

The rock house Grandpa built on his acre of the ranch was where Mommy grew up and where my parents would marry. Grandpa's house is remembered by cousins as the fun one where Grandma Ada Lee played ragtime piano and made the best lemonade on the ranch. Grandpa was a grizzled character in cowboy boots, and drinking partner to anyone in search of one. By the time I knew him he was legendary, equally at home working cattle on horseback or gunning his white Lincoln over the cattle guards of one of his ranches or chairing the Board of a bank in town.

Mommy, his firstborn, was in her second year of music studies at the local university when she and Dad met at a party. On his way to a MASH unit in Korea, his orders had changed at the last possible moment and he was sent down to San Antonio to install and operate one of the first artificial kidney machines. A Jewish Yankee from way up in New York, Dad was as alien a creature as ever stepped onto the ranch but redeemed to some extent by being a doctor and, even better, a democrat. Within days of their August meeting he and Mommy were writing stunning poetry to one another and by Thanksgiving they were husband and wife.

VII.

LIKE MOMMY, DAD WAS THE ATTRACTIVE AND GIFTED firstborn of three. Growing up, not much had been beyond his reach and he had sailed through school to enter Yale at sixteen. Because it was wartime the undergraduate programs were accelerated, and he was graduated in three years to begin medical school at Columbia before he was twenty.

Despite how things would fracture in time, at the start Dad and Mommy were wild about one another. An unsettling incident or two early on may have hinted to Dad of her problems, but he was undeterred. They may even have reinforced a sense he had that he was just the rescuer she needed. He had a justifiable confidence in himself and his analytic insight. A newly minted physician well read in psychiatry, he was ready and even eager to take on the physical and psychic ills of the world. Something in her

emotional fragility perhaps even inflamed in him a certain
ambition.

Several people who knew my parents have pointed out
the striking parallels between their relationship and that of
Dick and Nicole Diver in F. Scott Fitzgerald's *Tender is the
Night*. Dad himself used to comment on the likenesses. I
think he took a sort of pride in the comparisons and in the
notion of himself as the central character of a literary clas-
sic. But the story is a disturbing one about a psychiatrist
whose life is destroyed when he falls in love with and mar-
ries a patient. Both the novel and Fitzgerald's own marriage to Zelda Sayre, which inspired the book, were
described using the same terms—"a man of almost limitless
potential who makes the fatal decision to marry a beautiful
but mentally ill woman." How would Zelda have described
the tale, I wonder?

In college I would occasionally attend a small church
in my neighborhood and was surprised and moved one
Sunday to discover that Zelda herself was buried in the little cemetery behind the church. As a young teen I had read
Nancy Milford's biography of Zelda and had been haunted
by the rendering. There was something so familiar and
frightening to me in its echo of Mommy. Years later, long
after Mommy and Dad were both gone, I was tracing
Mommy's genealogy through her mother's line and there

she was—Zelda Sayre. Mommy's own cousin, and none of us had ever known.

After his discharge from the Army in 1952, Dad left Texas with Mommy and returned to New York to resume his medical practice in Westchester. He was back in this element in that county where he had lived all his life. Mommy, much younger and less secure, was stepping into a new and challenging time of life in an unfamiliar part of the country. Her life would progressively be overtaken by the demands of four children and husband, his career, numerous pets and a large house.

Her friends, themselves barely keeping things under control at home, confess now that they breathed easier in our messy house. But Mommy did not see that others were struggling as hard as she was. She considered it a private and singular failure all her own. She did not live long enough to see how many of her friends would themselves one day be strolling the lawns of the private psychiatric hospitals that dot that pretty county.

VIII.

WHEN WE WERE VERY LITTLE, THERE WERE PRIVATE JOKES between them, a loving look, a wink. She could defuse his tension with her teasing and light tone. She still had energy then and was willing to expend it on him. Early on she knew our favorite foods and tickle spots. There were dry mittens and our sandwiches were cut into stars or hearts. There was coconut cake on the kitchen counter. The bullseyes that fluttered from the tree branches out front were ones she had hand painted for our popguns and whiffle balls.

On Christmas, she would be on the floor with us marveling at the goodies, dressing the dolls, trying out the train, fanning the pages of new books, pointing out some overlooked treasure. Dad the detail man would be moving among us taking care of business, tightening bike pedals and installing batteries, assembling whatever we needed him to, eagerly intent upon providing the ideal Christmas for us all.

Dad was the one who tended the lawn and in summer it was he who would be in the pool with us and who taught us to swim. When the time came Mommy would lie alongside each one of us on the big four-poster bed to teach us to read. She liked the indoor things and those things close to home, reading and gardening, music, sketching and painting.

Low key as she was, suburban New York of the late fifties with its energy and striving could only have been bewildering at times. Success and satisfaction were measured so differently than they were at home in Texas. Where one had gone to school seemed to matter greatly. The wives attempting delicate crepes seemed not to miss good tortillas or ranch honey. No one was grateful for a soaking rain, they only moaned that it interfered with the Sunday sail or golf game. They surely could talk—these skinny eager young husbands could project and analyze and theorize and diagnose. But could any of them smell a coming storm? Could they mend a fence? Would they notice a half-buried arrowhead at their feet? The inner pockets of the well-cut suits on these earnest young men held expensive fountain pens and Kappa keys. Mommy alone seemed to know that life could get tangled and catch you at the ankles and would more often require a good pocketknife.

Her children were her rescue in a world unnerving to her. Usually harried, often overcome, she turned our way and reached for us. We were her comfort, her relief, and she was ours. She stood in each of our fearful child worlds as comfort incarnate. Our greatest solace was to have her near. And not content merely to touch her, we clung to any patch of her not yet claimed by a sibling. If we sensed her start to rise, our grips would tighten in dread. Every leave-taking was a tearful, prolonged agony to be gotten through, whether saying good-bye in the school parking lot or off to lunch with a friend. We held on as long as possible only letting go when we had to, when forced to disengage. And we were thrown back then into that unwelcome and confusing re-acquaintance with our own bodies, with where she ended and we began. A survey of boundaries that will continue our whole lives.

IX.

As PAINED AS DAD WAS BY MANY OF THE PARTICULARS of our home life, he did spend an inordinate amount of time recording and filming and photographing it. Perhaps he predicted the need we would soon have for exhibits of a former time when we had all been together. But whatever the reason, he often faced our family life from behind a camera lens shooting hours of home movies. In the ones that were shot outdoors his shadow is sometimes visible at our feet, one hand holding the camera to his eye, the other waving directions at us. In the movies shot indoors we squint in every shot, blinded by the hot bright light he had to use.

Each segment of the movie begins the same way. We look up suddenly, as if he had just called to us to look over here at the camera. Though the movies are silent you can imagine him saying, "Honey, can you smile for the camera?

Can you wave?" and in shot after shot, year after year, we comply, with less and less enthusiasm.

The hours of movies and audiotapes and the stacks of photographs bear witness to how faithfully Dad conserved and preserved moments of our lives for future consumption. Unable, perhaps, to face an experience as it was happening, he saved it up for later. He knew these were important days and events and relationships that should be considered, but not now. I am sure he wished a future day for each one of us when we would have better tools and a stronger back-up team than this meager sextet. And so he began a collection for his children of sample experiences and reactions. He tagged them like moon rocks and stored them away.

He often took the same photograph from every possible angle as if to be absolutely sure that a particular moment was not lost to us. Would that they were. Would that they could have been, that more of those moments had been lost to us, and we to them. We tried and we succeeded in being lost to many of the moments of our lives. Early in life we children learned to absent ourselves—we had excellent teachers in our parents. We developed our own ways of removing ourselves, and each one could disappear at will without leaving so much as a swinging door or a puff of smoke to signal our departure.

Sometimes when Dad was taking home movies he would set up the big tape recorder at the same time to capture the sound. The plan was always the same—to later synchronize the audiotape with the silent movies, but he never managed it. When we watched the movies, Mommy's smile would be on the screen but Nick's voice would be heard, or the sight of a tearful face would forewarn a coming wail, but by the time it was heard we would have moved on to a cheerier image. Dad tried time after time to match up sight and sound. And we would have to wait out those frustrated attempts before he would finally give up and re-thread the projector and allow us to watch the movies without sound.

Once he actually tape recorded the conversations we had among ourselves while we watched the silent movies. So a later evening was devoted to listening to audiotapes of our reactions to silent home movies, movies that had been filmed to record moments of our lives. We lived at some remove from our experience.

X.

MOMMY COULD TRANSFORM ABRUPTLY. OVERWHELMED by noise and chaos, the frantic look would come. I would know then we were about to lose her. The switch was always a frightful thing, the suddenness and totality of it. Her hands would fly up to cover her ears, pressing into her head as hard as she could, her eyes would squeeze shut and she would grind out of clenched teeth, "If only I could just *think!*" With that, the door to Mommy would slam in our faces.

I could never remember saying or doing anything to account for the switch, but my child mind took the blame whenever it happened. Perhaps my renegade mouth or hands were sending messages I knew nothing about. I didn't know how, but I seemed continually to be sabotaging my dearest wish, which was to keep her near, present in body and soul.

Sitting at her desk by the dining room window she

would sit staring and unmoving for impossibly long periods, her fountain pen or cigarette drooping between her fingers. I would watch, hesitant to call her back but afraid not to, knowing how her head would jerk with a start, how she would gasp and spin on me angrily. And so it was haltingly, guiltily, that we approached her at those times. She so clearly and dearly wanted to be let go. I always cringed at the ferocity with which she crashed back into our presence. We vowed to be better children, to be easier, to be quieter, to require less and still less.

She took the pills she was given to sleep, to wake up, to calm down. She moved through her paces in a dreamy daze. Sometimes she dropped to the floor in a faint wherever we were, the five-and-ten or the cleaners, and someone—the stock boy or the gas station man—would drive us home. One day in the stationery store I punched her thigh to force her out of the spaciness she was floating through beside me. "Stop it!" I whispered fiercely, yanking at her skirt, demanding her presence, afraid to be on my own so far from the house.

Back home again we children would be left to our own deficient devices while she absented herself. Her body would be physically present but she was out of it. She was sitting there on the couch, I could see her, I could touch her arm. But her glazed eyes held a different truth, and I was equally certain that she was not there at all. My eyes told me she was there but her eyes told me she was not. Which was true? Whose eyes to believe? She was there but she was not. She was the adult but she was one of us. She was with me but I was alone. All of these were true at once. And such simple fearsome contradictions as these forced me early on to mistrust not only her various messages, but the messages of my own sight and hearing and mind as well. I was under threat from within and without—within myself and without my mother. I learned to suspect all of my senses as liars and defectors in her probable employ. My senses, my mind itself, seemed to be operating out of loyalty to someone other than me.

I kept myself battle-ready by expecting disasters and anticipating impossible scenarios. I would plot a means of coping, endlessly talking myself through my best hope for survival. *If someone takes you to the beach and forces you to count all the grains of sand, just do it very slowly and you won't lose your place. And you can start all over if you get mixed up. ... If someone makes you walk to California all by yourself just don't look too far ahead, keep your head down. Go step by step, a little bit every day. Eventually it will be over.*

XI.

IT WAS THE ERA OF DR. SPOCK, AND THE BOYS AND I WERE never disciplined or restrained, and it showed. We were an almost feral lot, running wild and unsettled. No behavior was disallowed, no limits set on how far we could go in testing and tormenting one another, which made for tumultuous days. But the conflicts between us also likely resulted from our constant close proximity to one another. Early on we had begun to move as a group, to huddle together. There was strength in numbers. Watching TV, with the entire master bedroom to spread out in, we would scrunch together on one end of Mommy and Dad's four-poster bed. We tended not to venture too far individually, perhaps reasoning on some level that a multi-headed creature on eight legs would be harder to knock over than one of us alone. We felt safest when locked onto one another, even if the grip happened to be a choke hold. The animals were subjected to the same grasping need, and our basset hounds,

Wiggles and Freckles, Rochester the cat, and even the hamster were all squeezed and petted and loved nearly to death.

We did not let go easily—of each other, of pets, of baby bottles. We clung to whatever we had a handle on at the moment. Things came to be very important. Possessions could be carried around and kept in sight. Solid objects could be grasped, held, wielded, and trusted not to walk off. Dad prized his record collection. Mommy had a plastic cereal bowl on her dresser for years holding the curls from Toby's first haircut. We were perpetually in and out of her room and cupboards, and careless with her things, but that bowl was something we did not disturb. I was not too young to note and to be touched by how sentimentally she treasured those curls.

Nick and I were closest in age and probably looked the most alike of the four of us, the same shaped face and blue eyes and very blond hair. There is a family legend of the day he tried to give me away. I was two and had toddled out of the yard and into the road. When a car came barreling down the hill, the driver saw me and stopped. Carrying me into our driveway, he asked Nick, "Does this little girl live here?" and Dad stepped out of the house just in time to see Nick solemnly shaking his head from side to side.

Not that day, but on most days Nick was the truth in our midst. As Jess and I anxiously measured our steps and words, Nick would come barreling in, racing past, stopping at nothing, not even the glass French doors in the living room, which he once ran right through. He was the only one with the sense and the nerve to announce as loudly as behavior can that something was not right at our house. While the rest of us stood by, whistling, studying the ground or sky, Nick demanded action, response, rectitude. He howled for someone—anyone—to make a move, to take a stand, to do something.

Despite the tensions between us, the boys and I were protective of one another and there were occasions of genuine compassion. Our ride home from school involved a change of buses and I was inevitably asleep when the time came. But Nick daily helped me with the move, "Wake up. It's time to change buses. Gimme your lunch box." Suspicious at first, I softened quickly at his kind tone and welcomed with relief the intimation that life could hold wakings as gentle and generous as this.

XII.

IN LATE AFTERNOON, AS THE HOUSE BEGAN TO DARKEN, the boys and I would try rousing Mommy from the couch— first with kisses and whispers, then with impatient shakes. We once covered her with handfuls of daffodils collected from behind the house, but she slept on. After the boys disbanded I stayed behind and curled up in that narrow space between couch and coffee table, my head resting on her inert body. I watched the long fingers that I loved, so near now to my face, and willed them to rise up in a caress. I slid myself down to position my head right into her palm and stayed in that awkward scrunch savoring her touch—a laying-on of hands from which she was wholly absent.

Toby, two years younger and often my comfort, waddled in leaky and hungry and flopped down beside me. He seemed always to be wet, but the diaper pins were beyond me. There were red rings on his thighs where the rubber pants pinched. The milk in his baby bottle smelled sour. He carried his, and I mine, through our fourth or fifth years. I kept them filled for both of us.

Into the kitchen then to scavenge for dinner. Dragging a chair to the counter, I passed down crackers and peanut butter before reaching for the blender to whip saltines and plops of catsup and hot tap water into a tomato soup of sorts.

As evening became night and bedtime came and went, we grew noisy and rough, and tearful fights were likely to break out among us. We were weary. Nights were long in that house and not necessarily for sleeping. Mealtimes were not necessarily when food appeared. Adulthood was not necessarily a time to be an adult and childhood was not necessarily a time to be a child.

Things could change suddenly and by evening you had to learn to say not *President Kennedy* but *President Johnson.* Mommy could disappear and by evening you had to get used to saying not 'Mommy is up in her room,' but 'Mommy is gone for a while.'

When sleepiness finally would send me up the stairs, a bed squeaking and bumping against the wall would draw me to the doorway of Toby's room. I would watch him on his hands and knees rocking himself to sleep—forward and back, forward and back, soothing us both. I borrowed a bit of his comfort there as he sometimes borrowed my bottle when his had rolled under the couch and out of reach.

From his room I had to walk past the room Jess and Nick shared to get to my own. Beside their bunk beds a dresser had been built right into the wall. When no one was looking, Jess sometimes would slide out the bottom drawer and crawl through to the space behind, pulling the drawer in after him. He could fit back there and lay low between the walls of the house, hiding out in that netherworld between his room and another. I never knew where he had gone or how he could retreat to his room only to disappear into thin air, but it didn't surprise me. People often disappeared in that house. But the sound of harmonica music he left behind fed my growing certainty that Jess was a magical boy.

XIII.

THIRTY YEARS LATER I WOULD COME HOME TO A MESSAGE one day from a police detective in New York. Calling back, I was told he had left for the day but another officer tried to help. "What's this about?" he asked.

"I'm not sure. It may be about my brother, Jess Gordon. He lives in that area."

Well, let's see. We got a guy . . . We got a deceased at 154 Washington Avenue. That address mean anything to ya?"

Relief poured through me. "No! My brother lives at 150 Ft. Washington Avenue."

"That's what I said, lady."

"Oh."

"Look, I'll call ya right back. Lemme get the file in fronna me so we know what we're talkin' about."

My husband was at work and our son at school. I was home alone except for two women from a housecleaning service I was trying for the first time. Just as I hung up one of them came into the kitchen with a question.

"Would you stay here a second?" I asked her. "I think I'm about to get some bad news." I felt almost tenderly toward her as if I sensed we were about to become linked in some way, that she was going to be the witness to a fateful moment of my life.

"What's your name?" I asked her as the phone rang.

"It's Julia."

"Just stand here a minute, Julia, would you mind?"

As the officer talked I reached out and took her hand. "My brother's dead," I whispered, and Julia began to cry.

JESS HAD BEEN dead several days when they found him. And more days passed before they found me and let the family know. Then time was needed to positively identify the body. I helped the police track down dental records. After that a full week passed while the records were copied and delivered first to police and then to the coroner so a determination could be made. In the meantime, we waited.

There was a chance it wasn't him, wasn't there? We asked it of each other all week, and we asked it of ourselves. But alone and secretly we asked other things as well. *Haven't you prepared for this over the years? Haven't you expected such a call? When he was unreachable for weeks on end, weren't there times when you could only imagine that he was dead? Lying in bed at night haven't you sometimes planned his funeral after one of those calls of his that sounded like good-bye?*

The coroner called at last confirming that the body in that bed was sweet brother Jess, dead of an overdose. And I found of course, curled up and howling on my bed, that all the rehearsals for this moment had been wasted and no use at all. Nothing makes it real until it happens, and when it happens he is gone.

XIV.

BIG BROTHER JESS. SO OLD HE WAS AT FOUR YEARS BEYOND me. He did real homework and carried the book satchel my friends and I aspired to. He could shuffle cards and wiggle his ears. But there were things that were beyond even Jess. I had been so proud when he ran my sixth birthday party. I thought he was having a grand time hanging the prizes on the fishing poles that my friends and I gleefully flung over the side gate. He blindfolded us for pin-the-tail and manned the hi-fi for musical chairs.

It was only years later that I learned how angrily he had filled the pink treat baskets on the table and the goody bags that my friends had carried home. He had been playing at a friend's house when Mommy called him home to handle my party. He carried the Kool-aid and the cake that she was unable to cope with and he carried all the resentment and fear that they engendered.

The day after the coroner called I was on the phone

with the cemetery man in Texas discussing burial options. He concluded by telling me it would be possible, if we chose, for Jess to be buried in our mother's grave. Something seized in me at that suggestion and after hanging up I could only sit for a long while staring at the floor.

It was sometimes done, wasn't it—a child buried with his mother? Or was that only with infants? Jess was a grown-up. Grown-ups aren't buried with their mothers. Grown-ups are expected to stand on their own two feet, even in death, and be buried alone. But something in the notion kept resounding to me and by evening I had not yet let it go. That night when I called Toby I relayed it to him: *We can bury Jess in Mommy's grave.*

In the long silence that followed, the echo of what I had said came back to both of us. In that quiet clearing of time we came upon a truth never before put into words that in some way Jess already was buried with Mommy. He had been with her since the day she died.

Music and poetry formed the well-worn bridge between them. These were their means of exchange, their currency, their private language, two of the central strands of the complicated connection between them. Each was the firstborn, the soft-haired one, the dark-haired one, the artist. Each was the gifted one, the musical one, the sensitive one, the poet. When Jess was little, their similarities brought a sense of delighted recognition to those who knew them. But after she died when Jess was twelve, and as he grew from childhood into adolescence, his echo of her would become more weighted and ominous.

Jess brought Mommy to mind. He brought her in his sad face and in his dark hair. He brought her in his music, in his gentle nature, in his drinking. He brought her to every encounter and dropped her at our feet, all of us who had known her and loved her and were trying to be free. The enduring conundrum of Jess and Mommy is this: that he had emerged from her body and yet he managed to carry her within him for the rest of his life. She was a weight that he believed he had to bear in order to live and in the end the very weight that pulled him under.

The burial plot beside Mommy was available and that is where we buried Jess, at her side. It had been his place from the beginning, the spot he had never relinquished.

XV.

Mommy had taken Jess and Nick to Texas when I was two weeks old to be with her mother, who was dying of cancer. They were gone for six months and I was left at home in the care of a baby nurse. By the time they returned to New York the boys had had a long savor of Grandpa and the ranch. Jess was in chaps and holster, a confirmed Texan at age four.

Grandpa had been sending or bringing tokens of that world to homesick Mommy since before any of us had been born, and the packages continued throughout our childhood. Tins of ranch honey or molasses arrived by mail or in his suitcase when he visited. An arrowhead or a couple of fossils in a wooden cigar box would come cushioned in wadded pages from *Texas Cattleman*. Jars of the Mexican caramel sauce he had picked up in Laredo. He once sent a live horny toad in a boot box lined with buffalo grass.

We liked it best when he brought the goods in

person—he smelled wonderful, like his cigars, and patted our heads with a leathery hand. He talked to Mommy about the ranch, cattle prices, drought, politics. He and Dad exchanged jokes with bad words. Indoors he put his booted feet up on the furniture and outdoors he turned his head aside periodically to spit into the pachysandra.

Walking around that front lawn he would squat down to look the shrubbery dead in the eye. He would touch plants, shear off a stem, smelling, tasting, pointing with his knifepoint, explaining to us how water moved up from the roots to the leaves, while we shifted, bored, antsy to get away, to go in to Mommy, to the TV.

Grandpa remarried after Ada Lee died, and he brought Big Laura up to New York with him on his visits. She was much younger than Grandpa, only three years older than Dad, but she seemed older, she acted older. She dressed neatly and had big hair. We were paired from the start, whenever it was that one of the boys called her Big Laura or me Little Laura, designations that stuck. She was firm with us but affectionate and quick to laugh. I liked her unhesitant manner, how sure she was.

On Big Laura's lap one day when I was three I apparently asked her if she would be my mommy. She would tell me of it years later. "You already have a wonderful mommy," she answered. But something she saw during that visit must have caused concern because when she and Grandpa returned to Texas they took me with them, and I stayed with them for several weeks. She told me later she had wanted to offer Mommy some relief. And as I was not yet in school as the older boys were, but was older than Toby, still a baby, I was the easiest one to take with them.

After Mommy died, when false guilt would frequently send me scouring the past, most haunting to me would be moments like those on Laura's lap. It would seem to me that my betrayal of Mommy had been first sown there. Auditioning and casting understudy mothers. Was I securing provision for myself or rejecting Mommy's example? Perhaps it was both. Perhaps these were the first tentative, toddling, disloyal steps off the path that her life was illuminating for me.

XVI.

AT THE SCHOOL BUS STOP ONE AFTERNOON A CAR PULLS up to the curb and stops.

"I passed you before, honey. What are you doing there just standing by the road? Where do you live?" the lady asked me.

I didn't know how to answer. Without a house number I could only tell her that our house was over that way, up the hill. When she told me to, I got into her car and she took me to her house nearby.

"Why hasn't your mother come to get you?"

That was harder than "Where do you live" and I was silent. I could and did recite our phone number when asked, and off she went to call the house. When she returned, she said to her teen-aged daughter, "Can you imagine? Forgot her own daughter! Said, 'Oh! The boys are at a birthday party today. I forgot about her!' Not the least bit concerned that a stranger has her daughter!"

The lady's head shook from side to side a couple of times before the daughter's started too, and they exchanged a look before turning to me. I tried to think of something to say. I knew I should be offended on Mommy's behalf. I wanted to explain her behavior, to excuse it, to beg indulgence, but I sat wordlessly on their couch feeling ashamed of Mommy, ashamed of my silence.

I liked the way this mother and daughter stood together. Even as I searched for the words to defend Mommy, part of me wanted to walk over to where they were standing and to shake my head with them. Already I was struggling under the weight of a daughter's allegiance. I secretly wished Mommy would stand up straight and confidently lead. I got tired of keeping a step ahead. Sometimes I resented having to coax her along, to encourage her to continue, to watch for both of us where we set our feet.

But Mommy appeared at the door then, breathless and messy and embarrassed, and I jumped up in love and relief, grateful to grab hold of that familiar sweet hand and determined to get her out of there quick, away from those angry eyes sizing her up.

"Laura, you know I love you, don't you?" she asked me later. And I nodded in silence, ever cautious. Sometimes with Mommy the *I love you* had to be set aside untasted so that the urgent plea behind the words could be decoded and the correct response given. I could see in her face that my answer mattered greatly. She was asking for something, but as usual I didn't know what it was. Her *I love you* was the gift wrapping on a weighty box that was sometimes just too much trouble to open.

I sat in anxious silence. I would be unable to decipher the plea or I would answer it inadequately, and either way I would have failed her once again. Each crying jag, each dazed wander down a supermarket aisle, each ambulance trip down the driveway and out of sight, was an accusation that I took to heart.

XVII.

THE SOUND OF CAR TIRES SPEWING GRAVEL IN THE DRIVE-way at Doe Hill could signify either of my parents making their respective escapes to their respective hospitals, he in his sporty Sunbeam, she in the back of an ambulance. It was a snowy afternoon the first time I stood at an upstairs window watching my mother being lifted into an ambulance. She would be gone for months that time. Someone said she was going away for a rest. But why leave for that? She could rest at home, she rested a lot on the couch. And we could be quieter. *Don't go.*

They lifted the stretcher, and as they slid it into the back of the car her face was the first thing to disappear. I could see her from the neck down and then from the tummy down and then from the knees down, and then she was gone. They slid her in like a sweet cake raw and dangerous in its present state but one that would reemerge months later in a more nourishing form. In the meantime, in her absence, we would learn in new ways where she ended and nothingness began.

After she left we would come upon the tissues and envelopes she had used to blot her lipstick. The house was littered with those red kisses and we read each one as a warning flag from a phantom determined not to be forgotten. It was as if she feared the truth that we were just beginning to test—that it might hurt less to forget her than to miss her so much.

We kept an anxious eye on Dad now, following him from room to room. Lined up on the four-poster in the mornings, we were the hooting peanut gallery critiquing his form and echoing his grunts as he conducted his daily toe touches and deep-knee bends. Then everyone into the bathroom to study his shaving technique and to get an Aqua Velva splash before begging some of the icicles that hung outside the window. Enjoying an audience as he did, and tasting the new and fragile camaraderie between us, he mightily thrust up the window with a snarl, pretending to be Superman.

His playfulness delighted us and set off several moments of loud giddiness while his long arm reached from the warm steaminess out into the freezing air to grasp the ice and snap it off. He was careful to preserve the thrilling sharpness as he passed in one after another until each of us had our treat. We wrapped the fat end in a washcloth and wielded the frozen wand, alternately sword fighting and nibbling at the frozen point. When our mouths had chilled into cold red Os, we unwrapped what icy stalk was left and dropped it hard into the tub to watch it shatter, the pieces in a fast slide toward the drain.

That little bathroom of Dad and Mommy's was the site of a secret endeavor in which we children were joined. Whenever we received a bit of money as an allowance or from a grandparent we would make our secret way to this medicine cabinet. We would push aside the bottles and jars to reveal a secret bank. The little slot was just the size for our quarter or half dollar, and we slipped in the coin for safekeeping. We all threw in together, our riches combined. Though uncertain of the system of retrieval, we were confident that somewhere our treasure was held for us in safety. It is yet. Somewhere in the walls of that house our fortune lies. To a rusted hole in the wall intended for razor blades—dulled but still deadly and double-edged—we children entrusted our treasures.

XVIII.

O**N A SATURDAY IN WINTER DAD DROVE THE ENDLESS DRIVE** to Mommy's hospital. We all piled out of the car, shoving one another and dragging the mittens on yarn that hung out of our coat sleeves. As he signed in at the visitors' desk, Dad was reminded that children were not allowed on patient floors. He announced then in his radio-announcer voice that he was Dr. Gordon. But the nurse didn't care who he was, children were not allowed upstairs. Dr. Gordon cursed then and ran his hand through his hair and I waited, scared, to see what would happen next.

He called upstairs before shepherding all of us back outside. Squinting in the glare of sun on snow, we waved quickly chilling fingers at a high window at which stood a tiny figure that could have been Mommy. It could have been anyone at all.

Back to the car then for the whiny, hungry trip home. I didn't join the fight for the front seat. Instead I slipped in back to sit right behind Dad. I laid my head on his shoulder he was my captive as he drove. Humming, he absently reached up to pat my head. I saw a blimp for the first time that day. "GOODYEAR," it said. It was 1961.

Just before Mommy had left, Jess had found one of his Christmas presents in her closet. It was already wrapped and tagged and, unable to resist, he snuck it into the downstairs bathroom and tore off the paper. It was just what he had hoped, the camera kit he had asked for. He opened the box and spread the pieces out on the chilly tile floor and tried to make sense of it all, to fit it all together, to make it work. But he realized before long that he was alone with this; he couldn't ask for help with a gift he was not yet supposed to have. So he did the only thing he could think to do—he opened the bathroom window and dropped the camera piece by piece into the snow drift beneath the window.

There was a week in July when she came home for a trial run and then she was gone again. Dad's mother, our Meema, wrote to a friend, "As I see it, they are letting her stay home for longer periods each time and then return for therapy. The children are wonderful, 'though I can see they are a bit much for her."

We were, no doubt, a bit much for her. And she was a bit much for us. It sometimes seems we were left as much bereft by her life as by her death, as lonely for her in her presence, as deserted, as in her absence. I would grow accustomed to her being back home only to have her disappear once again. And when I no longer awaited her kiss at night, it would unexpectedly be delivered, re-igniting my hunger for it.

When finally Mommy came home for good, our joy at her return was tempered by the realization that she was not entirely with us. We led her by the hand to the couch, to our rooms, to her bed. She came back gradually, like a Polaroid, becoming sharper and more focused over time. In the early days she moved slowly through the house looking too intently at furniture and objects that had surrounded her for years. This mommy looked like ours, or at least a slow-motion version of ours, but she didn't know our birthdays or the dogs' names. This one got lost taking us to school and didn't recognize our friends. But we gratefully snuggled against this cozy, hollow look-alike while we waited for the real mommy to return.

XIX.

ONCE SHE CAME HOME FROM THE HOSPITAL, AFTER THE shock treatments and the pills and the experimental LSD treatments, she sometimes was elsewhere for stretches of time. Of course she was. She would try to report back from those dark jaunts with dispatches that always came without warning and always terrified.

She would smile and wave me over conspiratorially and I would scoot across the room and cuddle up close in delight. She would begin to speak quietly and I would lean in to catch every word, eager to share the secret. But her words would veer off into nonsense, no longer following one another in an ordered path, and my panic would flame up. She whispered soothingly about the milkman on the morning I was born, and about the stars that fell into the milk . . .

The seriousness of her expression, the earnestness with which she spoke made me sure that the problem must be mine. I wondered if I had missed something, the key that would make it all come together as sense. Was this that scary thing she did sometimes? Was it happening again? *It's happening again.* That was my phrase. That was the warning I sent out to myself in my head. *It's happening again.* That's how I armed myself and prepared myself and scared myself. Three words, and every system on alert.

She is still talking, and with urgency, and I begin to cry.

"Darling! What's wrong?"

"You're not making any sense," I whimper.

Injured protests then, and a cold tone. But of course she was making sense. What was I so upset about? Stop this right now!

Each time it happened I agonized over my choice—to try to reason with her and incite her anger, or to nod and agree with whatever she said. Either way she was lost to me. Most often I nodded in silence. It ended more quickly that way. But each time I did so, I hated myself for it. And I hated her for forcing me to conspire in her truancy, for making me hold the door while she fled us.

One evening as Dad came in from work, he caught me up in a hug in the upstairs hallway and I announced a little too loudly into his neck, "I love you more than her."

"Shh! She'll hear you," he answered, alarmed, turning quickly to make sure she wasn't within earshot.

"I don't care," I told him defiantly, tired of her fragility and feeling brave in his arms. I hoped she would hear me. I was out of sympathy that day and felt only impatience at her refusal to snap out of it. But Dad's silence was not what I had expected. I thought it was a gift I was handing over. This was my pledge of allegiance. I was on his team now, wasn't he happy? Mommy was the one I wanted to hurt. But my words had backfired somehow and had consigned Dad to an anguished acre far from me. What to say, what to say, to bring him back? I had torched my bridges, left and right. There was only his hand distractedly, rhythmically patting my back, as unsatisfying and insufficient in its own way as her *I love you.*

XX.

1963 HAS BEEN CALLED AMERICA'S LAST SUMMER OF innocence and it was our last summer together as a family. We spent summer weeks at the beach and that year it was Rhode Island. On those trips Mommy passed along to us her passion for the sea. She loved to be near the water. Her clothes were looser and her hair was down. She was freed of something there. Like the other fathers, Dad stayed home to work and came up to join us on the weekends. His absence likely had a share in her calm.

Friends came to the little Rhode Island house to visit, some I didn't know. There was a Mrs. Martin for a few days with a young son. Or perhaps Martin was his name. They were in our bathroom one morning as I passed by, the mother standing beside her boy and brushing her own teeth as he brushed his. She stopped her brushing to gently correct his side-to-side strokes. I stood in the doorway watching in the mirror until she caught sight of me. She wheeled then and came toward me in a quick stride, a small insincere foamy smile around the words, "we don't like people watching us," and closed the door firmly. I wasn't spying, I wanted to protest. I just like the closeness. I was enjoying the sweet moment, her kindly correction of him. But the shut door stung me, as did the image in retrospect of that boy on our stepstool alongside a vigilant mother.

On beach walks Mommy explained the tides to us, pointing out the continual movement of the waterline. We climbed over jetty rocks to collect mussels. We poked and dug and raked for clams with our serene guide, her hands without tremor. We gathered seashells and sea glass under her tutelage. She described how time and salt and sand together worked to blunt sharp glass shards and make of them something beautiful and soothing to the touch.

She set up her easel by a window to sketch and paint. With a stick of charcoal on a clean page she would compose a quick clear sharp image only to reach up then to rub at it, to soften it, her hand darkening with the task. Her crisp lines became dreamy and blended together with only a hint here or there of outline, of bold stroke.

But there was a day of bold stroke, and it is one I have never forgotten. Jess and Nick had been playing too intently out on beach rocks to notice the incoming tide. A rock surrounded earlier by soft sand now stood in deepening water and the boys were trapped on its surface.

I made for the house, screaming for Mommy, fervently hoping I could wake her if she was on the couch. But before I even got to her she was out the door and speeding past me toward the boys, kicking aside her shoes and dropping her sweatshirt as she ran. Throwing herself into the water, she was out to the rock in no time. She brought Nick to shore first and pried his arms from her neck to return for Jess.

We had early learned to swim, and the situation was likely not as treacherous as it appeared to us then. But what remains as thrilling in memory as it surely was that day in reality is the unaccustomed taste of our mother's power when wholly focused—the speed of her run across the sand, the determination of her great splash into the surf, the strength of her voice calling out to her children in loud reassurance.

XXI.

Jess discovered a new passion that summer at the feet—the literal tapping feet—of Pete Seeger at the Newport Folk Festival of 1963. There had been several years of piano lessons by then, and music and books already were becoming as essential and central to him as they were to Mommy. But this was something new—Seeger's fingers flying over the strings of his guitar and banjo, all the while blowing on his harmonica or throwing his head back to sing out. When he wasn't performing, Seeger spent his free time where we did, at the home of his long-time friends and Mommy's cousins, Jessie and Harvey.

Bob Dylan was introduced that summer at the Festival by Joan Baez, already a family favorite for her early records and the slight resemblance she bore to Mommy. But here she was in the flesh, and Dylan beside her, and especially Seeger himself. And with all of them together, a boy's life was changed and a course was set and a door flung open as

Jess heard the folk-poets, the unpretentious expression of soul through poetry and fingers on strings.

After we got home that summer Grandpa bought Jess his first guitar. And from that time we would never again think of Jess without thinking of his guitar. That first one, like all the ones to follow, became an extension of Jess's body, a part of who he was. He had found his harbor.

Jess skidded into the kitchen one Friday in November yelling that President Kennedy had been shot in Texas. "Oh! What a horrible, horrible thing!" Mommy cried as she hurried past us up to the bedroom and the TV. She stayed there all weekend, crying, and we were in and out of the room watching with her.

I thought Kennedy's death was a private crisis all our own. Unlikely things happened in our family and I thought this was ours too. I planned to share the news when school resumed on Tuesday, and I was genuinely surprised to hear classmates discussing the death when I arrived that day. I wondered how they knew.

The funeral had been the day before. Watching the horse without rider, which seemed always on the verge of bolting, I had worried that it would. And I was afraid those backward black boots in the stirrups would fall to the ground. Caroline, just my age and coloring, held the hand of her mother, Mommy's age and coloring. As the two of them stepped up to the flag-draped coffin and knelt to-gether I wondered if Mommy and I would ever move to-gether so prettily, so quietly, in such unity.

Mommy was struggling and was sleeping more and more during the day. *Noche* was her nickname from child-hood, Spanish for *night*. Grandpa said she had been awake a lot during the night as a baby. And she was awake a lot during the night now. She seemed to have her days and her nights mixed up from the beginning and to the end.

Thanksgiving came. Christmas came. Winter came. And with them, longer and louder arguments. Yelling and tears and slammed doors. Fights over who was failing whom. She got slower and he got louder. And around and around and around.

XXII.

Mommy was a classroom helper at our school that last year. She expected to be late one morning and asked me to let her teacher know. Bursting with self-importance, I checked in with my own teacher and explained my mission before setting off on a proud march to Mommy's classroom. I knocked eagerly on the door, which swung open to reveal none other than Mommy herself, not late after all. I was so surprised at the sight of her, and so disappointed at not having the chance to deliver my message, that I started to cry.

She fell to her knees in tears and clasped me to her, begging me to explain myself. My minor disappointment was quickly subsumed by her larger panic. And in the face of her anxiety I had the sense not to stomp my foot and demand, as I wanted to, "What are you doing here?" She seemed not to remember my assignment, and I could think of nothing to say to explain either my presence at her classroom or my tears. Had she been less late than expected?

Had she never intended to be late at all? Had this all been an elaborate test of some kind? Was she tricking me?

I stood silent as reactions piled up in my mind—fear and anger and disappointment. Danger seemed to lurk in every verbal direction, potential misunderstanding and hurt feelings hid behind any words I might choose.

"Nothing, nothing," I offered lamely, unable to explain. Finding the right words was so complicated. I turned toward my classroom and walked away without looking back. I knew the look on her face by heart. But leaving her confused was preferable to leaving her hurt. And leaving her confused was preferable to her leaving me. The words that might have reassured her would more likely have launched us both onto a semantic minefield. My silence was the calculated choice of a child accustomed to difficult and lousy choices.

On an afternoon soon after, I heard her giving Elizabeth, the cleaning lady, a disjointed and senseless explanation as to why she couldn't be paid that week, and I was ashamed of us. After Mommy left the room I watched Elizabeth lower her head a moment. Maybe she gave her head a quick shake. Maybe she muttered something. Traveling through my early years alongside my mother I was pained by the expressions we left in our wake.

The end came one evening with a commotion in the

dining room. Nick was in tears with Mommy and Dad nearby. Dad beckoned me in, and Jess came too, and somebody went upstairs for Toby who came down with his hair still drippy from the tub. He reached up for a lift onto Mommy's lap and I settled onto Dad's. I just fit under his chin and was leaning against his chest when he told us that he and Mommy were getting a divorce.

"From this point onward there is no sane or protected place for this family." I once read that line about the family in *Tender is the Night* and I have never forgotten it. In the dining room that night we were not told much of what was to come. Who knew, after all? Mommy was about to enter the hospital for the last time and the six of us were only days away from settling into five different households, in three cities, in two states. I would not see the house being packed up and I don't remember leaving it. My memories of our family in that house end with that night, around that table, my father's tears collecting on my head.

Mercury

I.

IN THE MATTER OF GORDON VS. GORDON, *SCHEDULE A* WENT on for pages listing damages to the house in Mount Kisco and the costs of repairing them. It included such items as "16 glass panes installed," "pool repair—5 coats cement," "kitchen range repair," "replacement of kitchen and bathroom floors," "scrubbing of bathroom tiles," and item #9, "repair and repainting of picket fence."

Schedule B listed thirty-five outstanding debts around town from dog licenses and school tuition to milk delivery and extermination and hospital bills. Less tangible debts and damages would take longer to tally.

There was a plan in place by which all of us would leave Doe Hill and ease into a new chapter of life. Dad was to rent an apartment close to work and the rest of us were going to settle into a Connecticut farmhouse in nearby New Milford. We even spent a day there picnicking with Mommy in a field near the house. Gesturing with her sandwich, she stretched out an arm to indicate what we would do over there and there and there. She conjured a future of bright light and open space and being outdoors together. There would be animals and a garden and a playroom in the barn. We would move in when school let out for summer.

But we were never to see the farm again. Our life together ended sooner than planned, and differently. On the day the separation agreement was signed, Mommy broke down at school and had to be hospitalized. Aunt Rowena came up from Texas to care for us and to help Mommy get ready to go. She would be moved to a hospital in Texas to be closer to her father and sisters.

It was arranged for us children to go along to Texas with Aunt Rowena to visit with relatives for a few weeks to give Dad a chance to prepare the house for sale and to figure out the next step. But before we left, on our last Saturday in New York, Aunt Rowena took the four of us into Queens to visit the New York World's Fair. We stood in a long line to see Borden's Elsie the cow. We ate belgian waffles and heard a mechanized Lincoln recite the Gettysburg Address. We raced each other through the Kodak exhibit and cooled our heels in the fountain under the big hollow unisphere.

Late in the day we stood in one final line that led to a

moving walkway. We were going to see the Pietà. I loved the sound of the word and kept repeating it to myself, it was one we had been hearing all day. *Pietà*. "Michelangelo was the greatest sculptor of all time," Aunt Rowena told us as we waited in line. And this is one of his most famous sculptures. You're going to see Jesus with Mary, his mother."

What did I expect to see? A baby, I suppose, cradled in his mother's arms. But here instead was a long, grown man. He lay across Mary's lap and it was clear he was dead. I saw Mary's sad face and the way she held Jesus and was looking at him. I studied them, thinking it through. "That's her little boy," I remember explaining to myself. "He's a grown-up, and he's dead, but he's still her little boy."

II.

Whe day came, dad drove the four of us to
La Guardia, and Mommy and Aunt Rowena met us there.
We were excited at the prospect of a plane ride ahead and
very happy to see Mommy again after her several weeks in
the hospital. I imagine we paid Dad scarce attention and
delivered what were likely careless kisses as we anticipated
a brief separation from him. Unbeknownst to any of us,
more than a year was to pass before we returned to New
York or lived with either of our parents again. But on that
day all we knew was that we were going to Texas and we
were going with Mommy. She would lead us into the Promised Land, Grandpa country, her heartland.

Grandpa was the one who wanted her back in Texas
where she belonged and he had dispatched Aunt Rowena
to get Mommy discharged and to bring her home. But there
had been delays and disagreements at the hospital—the
bills had not been paid. "Your father has a bad history of

paying bills," the women were told. Grandpa would agree to pay, he always agreed, he liked to be needed. But when he didn't consider Mommy improved enough to justify the charges, he would toss the bills aside in contempt of the whole psychiatric profession.

We stopped in Houston and Big Laura got on the plane to accompany us children on the last leg of our trip to San Antonio. And sometime during that brief layover long forgotten now, Mommy kissed us good-bye and stepped off the plane and out of our lives.

On our first night in San Antonio, Toby went with me to Grandpa and Big Laura's house while Jess and Nick moved in with Aunt Jane. Our visit would be extended once and then again and again. We would switch houses every ten days or so, and I was sometimes with one of the boys or two or all three and sometimes none. Grandpa's house had the advantage of Big Laura. Rowena's house had a baby cousin to play with. And Aunt Jane had two tree-houses and had bins and cupboards filled with art supplies. She and her two children were living in the rock house that Grandpa had built years before and where she and Mommy had grown up, though the surrounding ranch was long gone by now. The city had spread out and the house was in the middle of a suburban neighborhood.

Texas, though strange to us, was marvelous—open

and flat and dusty. The houses had stucco walls and tile roofs and banging screen doors. In the yards were yucca plants and pecan trees. Hummingbirds whizzed by and we picked figs. The air blew hot but the wind smelled good. Something sweet was growing in San Antonio. The food was messy and I liked all the new things—enchiladas and grits and Dr. Pepper. "Goldwater for President" signs were everywhere and so were Dairy Queens and pick-up trucks.

By summer's end the boys and I had been in each of the relatives' houses and in every combination. We couldn't have Mommy, but we could have her family for a time. We could visit where she was most at home, where she felt most herself. We could savor the tastes and breathed in the scents that she liked best. We could play and nap and lie awake in the dark in the rooms of her childhood home.

III.

WHEREVER WE WERE DURING THE WEEK, THE BOYS AND I usually spent weekends together at Esperanza, Grandpa's ranch two hours south of town. We would ride down with Big Laura. Grandpa sometimes came with us but usually he was already down there. The landscape, as we drove, was flat and empty. A single tree stood out here or there with great spaces between. There was barbed wire and chaparral. Buzzards circled overhead.

It would be good to see the boys at first, a relief to be together again. But before long we would likely be jostling for position in the hot car. Once that started Big Laura would start a sing-along, gaily admitting she "couldn't carry a tune in a bucket." After an hour or so she would pull over to stretch her legs and to pour us lemonade out of the ice chest. "That hits the spot!" she would announce, smacking her lips and flinging the last drops out of her Dixie cup and into the scrub. Her cup was neatly labeled with her name, as all of ours were. She would collect them and wipe them out with a tissue and restack them for next time.

Back into the car then and more flat open space. Pickups went by, raising dust. The drivers wore cowboy hats and raised a finger off the steering wheel in greeting as they passed. Some had a cigarette in hand, all of them had guns hanging behind their heads. None of them looked like Dad. None of it looked like New York.

When the ranch was finally in sight, we argued over whose turn it was to open the main gate. Crossing over the cattle guard we passed under the black arching sign announcing 'Esperanza Ranch—Black Angus Cattle.' "Esperanza means hope," Big Laura liked to remind us.

We passed Joe's house first. He took care of things when Grandpa was in town. Long stretches then through pastures, past horses and longhorn herds and the three burros Grandpa had brought up from Mexico years before. They were good watchdogs, he told us. They kept coyotes away from the stock. Big Laura would go slow slow slow when we passed any of the cattle, looking them over. She always checked the stock tanks as we passed to see how much water there was.

At the house at last we pulled into the carport with its tangle of bridles and tools and antlers. Yapping dogs ran up to the car to greet us and scare us. These were working dogs and sometimes mean. Nothing like our slow sweet Wiggles and Freckles back home.

The main house was to the right of the carport and everything else to the left—the bunkhouse and trucks, cattle pens, tack room and barns. As we carried bags and boxes in from the car, weird string-beany pods hung overhead from mesquite tree branches and burrs snagged at our socks. Big Laura would be warning us again about the cacti and electric fence. All weekend, ever on the look-out for snakes and scorpions, I would be muttering the Texas words I was trying to remember. My sneakers were now *tennis shoes.* Toys didn't get put away they got put *up.* If I did something mean I was acting *ugly.* And it seemed there were no more g's on anything anymore. The boys and I now were eatin', sleepin', goin' places.

IV.

THE MAIN HOUSE, SCREENED ALMOST ALL THE WAY AROUND, was shaped like a wishbone. Antlered heads looking down on us from the walls were mostly deer, but there was also a fierce-looking javelina with teeth bared. That one had a happy red bandanna knotted around its neck. The furniture was rawhide, tanned skins stretched taut over wood frames. There were Navajo rugs "and have-a-heart" mouse traps scattered across concrete floors. On the way to our rooms we would pass Grandpa's big hammock and the bookcases loaded with books and family pictures and scattered arrowheads.

Out in the yard up on a high pole was the birdhouse for the purple martins. It was so high we thought it must be one of Grandpa's jokes, like the javelina. Hummingbird feeders hung from tree branches around the yard. If we could lie still enough on the lawn beneath the feeders the hummingbirds would hover just above us and feed.

When the big bell rang calling the cowboys to meals, I would cross the yard to the cookhouse. I liked to watch the cowboys come over from the pens and wash up at the little sink outside. Each one scraped his boots on his way inside and hung his hat on a chair post. The huge lazy Susan in the center of the table spun to the left and the right as they reached for the platters and serving bowls. They piled their plates high with biscuits and molasses, beans and tortillas and meat. They *yessired* and *yes, ma'amed* if spoken to, but mostly they just gobbled up their food and drank their ice tea in huge gulps. I watched them through the screen door, studying the boots, the spurs, the hats, and those bouncin' adam's apples.

There was a buckboard wagon out in the yard but we weren't allowed to play on it, it was too old. Noisy cicadas were everywhere and we stuck their brittle shed bodies to the front of our shirts. Grandpa kept the small metal kiddie pool in the side yard filled for us but out beyond the pens was the real pool, the old pool, empty for years. We were tempted to race down its sloping sides, but Grandpa warned us that snakes tended to nest under the brush that collected in the corners.

Big Laura made all of us lay down for a nap after lunch. The weather was too hot to do anything else and by that time of day she was worn out. We were a handful and she used to cry from tiredness, she told me years later. There were nights that summer when she cried out not to God above or to Grandpa beside her, but to Ada Lee, our dead grandmother. "Where are you?" she would demand. "Why did you leave all this to me?"

Sometime that summer it was decided and arranged for us to remain in Texas for the upcoming school year. Grandpa rented a house in town for the boys and me, and hired tiny, tough Mrs. Haslett to take care of us. She was already near seventy but undaunted by the assignment. Her hair and her Chevy were the color of steel, and like Big Laura she was kind and clear and not afraid to take charge. By the time school began, she and the boys and I all were moved into a new house and were ready to begin our year together at 444 Lellen Lane.

V.

THE HOUSE WAS A ONE-STORY CRAFTSMAN, STURDY AND square, with a sunporch in back where the boys slept. We would sometimes come home from school to find Big Laura or Grandpa had stopped by to check on us. Mrs. Haslett and Grandpa would sit in the kitchen over coffee and recite the long poems they had learned during childhood lessons at the very start of the century. It was always a happy sight to see Laura's car or Grandpa's white Lincoln in the driveway.

His car was natural history exhibit on wheels with plant cuttings and a bag of pecans on the seat and scattered cedar cigar boxes that might contain cigars or just about anything else—a rattlesnake rattle, flints, twine. The floor would be littered with papers, a rain gauge, lengths of fence wire. A hunk of chewing tobacco would be broiling on the dash. Under the front seat bottles clinked against a stray antler or nestled alongside the muzzle of his .22.

Big Laura brought over school supplies—Big Chief writing tablets for me and a bottle of Brasso for the big boys. Nick and Jess were in school at the local military academy for fourth and sixth grades respectively, and their uniforms were dazzling to me. In the evenings they shined their shoes with the shoeshine kit Mommy had sent them and they polished their buttons and belt buckles. Neither of them liked the school, but they did like marching band practice. Jess had taken up the trumpet and Nick played the drums.

Years later Mrs. Haslett would confide that Nicky had always been her favorite. She liked his spirit and energy and daring. And unsettled as he had been by the rapid succession of changes in recent months, his energy and daring were much in evidence that year. So much so that we came home one afternoon to find his things being packed up and to be told he was going to be going away to school. Big Laura said how much better it would be for him and for all of us, but we didn't like the sound of this. We didn't want anyone else to disappear.

Toby was in kindergarten at a church school nearby and he would spend every day of that year on the floor under his school desk, watchful and silent, in perfect and bewildered silence.

In the afternoons after school, Jess sometimes cried in

the backyard. He missed Dad and worried about Mommy and Nick. He felt responsible for all the rest of us and wondered what was ahead and when we would be together again.

My own school was near the house and I walked. Coming up our hill one afternoon I saw a pair of saddle shoes on the sidewalk and I stopped to look them over. Bending down for a closer look, I saw socks coming out of the shoes and legs coming out of the socks. It took me an instant to realize those shoes and socks and legs were my own. I straightened up then in embarrassment and looked around quickly to make sure no one had seen me stop. I started on my way again then, thinking through my discovery and what this could mean. *People can see me when they look.*

VI.

MOMMY GOT OCCASIONAL WEEKEND PASSES AND CAME for a visit two or three times that year. Dad flew down for the weekend every six weeks or so. When either of them was visiting, they would sleep in Mrs. Haslett's room and she would go to her son's place. It always took a little time to get used to being with Mommy or Dad again. We had to relearn their faces, the expressions and habits, the fit between us.

A bathroom connected my room to Mrs. Haslett's and I considered it my private access to whichever parent was visiting. But it also served as my hideaway. I liked the smallness of the room and the coolness of the floor tile, and it was where I sometimes went to play dolls undisturbed. Once, during a visit of Mommy's, I went in to rinse spilled juice off my hands and lingered a few minutes. I had closed both doors and was reveling in the quiet and the sense of safety and containment the room always gave me. "You really are alone," I told myself in the mirror. "Nobody's coming. Nobody's coming." Mommy banged in at just that moment and I screamed in surprise, running out past her.

It was something to laugh over but I was embarrassed and couldn't have explained what I had been up to. So I left her in one more doorway probably apologetic and certainly perplexed. And likely wondering, yet again, as I disappeared from sight, what in the world had just passed between us.

Mommy also went for visits with Nick. His school was not far from her hospital. On one of Dad's visits we went to see Nick too. The drive from San Antonio was long and took us all the way to the coast. Nick showed us around his school and then Dad checked us all into the Sand Dollar Motel for a weekend at the beach.

In the car on Sunday night, as we got back to his school, Nick started to cry and asked if he could go home with us. We didn't go with him to his room. We said goodbye on the sidewalk and staff members urged us to leave quickly. "Don't turn around. Don't turn around," Dad snarled as he hurried us into the car. He sounded angry and I didn't know why. We all were crying by then and hating ourselves for leaving, for not taking him with us, for not looking back.

When summer came, we left all of it—Nick, Mommy,

Grandpa and Big Laura, Mrs. Haslett, the ranch, and all those Texas words I had mastered. Big Laura put Toby and Jess and me on a plane when school ended and we went back to New York and to Dad. It had been several weeks by then since we had seen him and I studied his face as we left the terminal. His nose was bigger than I remembered. "You look like Danny Thomas," I announced, and he laughed all the way to the car.

He drove us that night to another rented house and another woman hired to care for us. This one was young and resentful. This one had a husband in prison and a toddler in tow and wanted to be anywhere but caring for us. She spent her afternoons in her room and we knew enough to stay out of her way. This one was using our phone to take and place bets for her bookie and was with us until she was arrested in the spring.

VII.

THE BOYS AND I PLAYED WITH THE TOYS WE FOUND IN that house but we were careless with them. We pulled books off the shelves and opened them wide, defying Dad's elaborate and reverent demonstrations of how to open good books only partway to spare the binding. I lay claim to whatever dolls I came across, renaming each one and endowing them with new life stories. The bedroom where I slept was filled with another girl's books and toys, and hinted at an attentive mother with a flair for decorating. I read with a flashlight at night under that girl's bedspread and matching sheets.

Dad was dating by now, and this would be the first we would see of that. He sometimes brought his dates to the house after dinner and would introduce us before they disappeared into the living room shutting the pocket doors behind them. There was one woman he saw for months. Mary had three big, crew-cut, unsmiling sons. They sometimes came over together on Saturdays. I liked Mary very much but I worried about all those boys. Six brothers would be several too many for me.

Mommy wrote to us regularly, and always Dad urged us to answer promptly. But I put it off as long as I could. When finally I did answer, I would put the most minimal effort into trying to keep her up on my life and interests and activities and friends. I would turn over her letters and answer each of her questions with a yes or a no. I added as few words of my own as I could manage before returning her letters to her. It was fast and it was mean but I missed her less if I gave her less thought. She belonged now to a place called Austin and I belonged for the moment to a house of someone called Geller.

We had classmates over to play with all the toys we found in that house. But I liked better to go to my friends' houses. I would play with them for awhile but then I would go off in search of their mother. I liked to watch the mom at her tasks and to talk. My friends got impatient with me and one of them once called me on it. "You come over to play with my mom, not me."

On those treks to the laundry room or kitchen I sometimes garnered an endearment. *Darling* was my very favorite, but rare. *Sweetheart* was more common and my friend Debby's mother called me *Honey*. The bottom of the barrel in my book was *dear,* so colorless and seeming to require so little of the sender. But I was not choosy and I hungrily gathered up whatever was uttered in my direction.

Sunday evening after Disney was when Mommy called, and the boys and I would get on different extensions. Things always began well enough but inevitably Jess would get interrupted, or I would prompt Toby or something else would cause tempers to flare or spirits to sink and things would fall apart. *I miss you, Mommy.*

"Now, don't cry, children," she would say. "Don't make me cry." Tears made the rounds then of the corners of the house, upstairs and down, until each of us hung up, Mommy included, desolate in our various rooms.

VIII.

I DOVE INTO BOOKS THAT YEAR. I LIKED WORDS, TO READ them and print them out. My teacher, Miss Hassell, kept me supplied with books she thought I would like. She smiled when I told her about the friend I had found in the letter *a*, a girl my age always in profile with a flip hairdo. I read and reread a book on Helen Keller and memorized the manual alphabet, which was printed inside the back cover.

Mommy came up from Texas for a visit in the spring. Dad went to stay elsewhere but he stayed home long enough to greet her arrival. We had not seen Mommy and Dad together for almost two years by now and something in me rose up in relief and joy when she came into the house and I watched them approach one another. But, drawing near, both reached out a hand for a crisp, quick handshake and I began to cry.

After Dad left we showed her around the house. We

took her to each of our rooms, pointing out our respective treasures. She petted my guinea pig and admired my Girl Scout uniform. She promised to sign my new autograph book.

There were changes in her that we tried to look past and to reassure ourselves about. The long hair I loved was gone. She had a tummy now. We kept searching out the familiar, looking in another spot when an old one failed to serve. There was that same smile and those two teeth that overlapped. She was wearing her bamboo bracelet like always.

We were each going to have a night of our own with her during the visit and we could choose to spend it with her at home or over at the Kittle House, the local inn where she was staying. Toby opted for the Kittle House and he and Mommy went off for their evening, hand in hand. For a long time afterward whenever we drove past the inn, Toby would announce, "There's Mommy's hospital!"

When the time came for my evening with her, I was still undecided and worried. I wanted Mommy to myself but I had a secret and no one to tell: I was afraid to be alone with her. I was afraid she would start to act scary and I wouldn't know what to do. So in the end I said I would rather stay home. I could see she was surprised and hurt. It wasn't true and she knew it. "Are you sure?" she kept asking, confused by my choice. No, I wasn't sure but I didn't know what else to do. I had been looking forward to our evening as much as she had been, but this seemed to be the only choice possible. And there was no way to explain it.

The boys were surprised but delighted by my choice. It gave them more time with her. As they made a grab for her hand to appropriate her for games and stories, I released her to it. "Go ahead. I don't care," I said, caring deeply. I sat apart all evening seething at their intrusion and hating myself for my choice.

I was with her but cut off. Longing for her but leery of her. Fearing what I most wanted and wanting what I most feared.

IX.

WE LEFT THAT HOUSE IN SUMMER AS WE HAD LEFT THE one before. Dad reminded us to put things back the way we had found them months earlier. We left the jigsaw puzzle unassembled as if we had never accomplished it. Doll clothes straightened, bedspreads smoothed. Books back onto shelves as if we had never dragged an eye or finger across their lines of type. We checked under beds for toys and socks. We gathered up our things. Floors were mopped, surfaces dusted, cracks filled in and we were gone.

Nick was still living away at school, and the rest of us—Jess, Toby and I—were going down to Austin to spend the summer with Mommy. She had been awarded custody in the divorce and now that she was out of the hospital this was intended perhaps as a practice run to see how she coped with caring for us.

Texas is far from New York and it was farther in those days. We left on a Tuesday and Dad had to work so his sister, our Aunt Peg, took us to the airport and saw us off. Children traveled without adults less often back before the national divorce rate took off, so there was a lot of chat between Peg and the flight attendants as they got us buckled up and settled in.

Kissing us good-bye, Peg dropped a treat into each of our laps for the long flight. Forty-five years later I still have mine—a blue plastic maze with a silvery blob of mercury inside. The objective is to get the mercury into the middle compartment without it coming apart. When it touches the walls too hard, it breaks into a million, shaky fragments. If that happens it all has to be handled with a light touch and the lid gently tapped to coax the silver bits back together into a cohesive whole. One little piece making it to the safety of the middle doesn't count. It all has to arrive together.

We arrived back in Texas a year after we had left. Mommy's apartment was the upstairs of a duplex. *Duplex* was a new word to me, one I liked the sound of. It was almost as good as *mentholatum*—a word I had first heard with delight not long before. The apartment had two bedrooms and baths. Mommy's piano was in the living room. The old bunk beds stood in the boys' room. Odd to see our old furniture in these new unfamiliar rooms. Many of our things had been in storage for years, including our familiarity with Mommy herself. We were eager to be at ease with her, to reconnect. In those first days she couldn't make a move in any direction without bumping into one of us. We slapped each other off to stand closest to her, to take her hand, we searched her face. Her hands were puffy now, floppy and loose. They didn't look as if they could fly across the keys of a piano. It was worrisome.

We wanted to feel safe. We wanted to feel the constraints of someone's fierce vigilance. But she was a bit slow in turning toward us when we spoke, a beat behind in smiling or composing a response. She sat looking out the living room window for a long while, her cigarette burning closer and closer to her fingers. We kept nervous watch ready to swoop in with the ashtray, suddenly remembering how it was with her, how watchful we needed to be. We wondered how she had managed without us.

X.

THERE WAS A DISTRACTED AIR. THE ANXIOUS LOOK ON her face was contagious. She was a bit unsteady on her feet, off balance. Stepping out the front door she stopped for a moment, her hand on the doorknob, as if to collect herself before facing the brightness of the day.

Dad would call to see how we were doing and to ask, "Is it great?" Yes, we parroted, it's great. His tone and wording gave away the answer he wanted and it was easy to get it right. Besides, we had not yet worked out in our minds exactly why it wasn't great. After all, this was where we thought we had wanted to be for two years—living with Mommy again, seeing her every single day. But it was not as we had imagined. It was not cozy or easy. She said she was happy but she acted sad. A look crossed her face, an odd little gesture stood out, and I remembered things.

The boys had their room and I slept with her in the old four-poster from Doe Hill. In the evenings she and Toby and I would line up on the bed and Jess would read us a story. Toby was seven that summer and I was almost nine. The book Jess read was about a runaway boy alone in the mountains, hunting and foraging and providing for himself. The author was a family friend and lived near us in Chappaqua. But I found the tale unsettling and couldn't make out why the boy was out there alone or why he would want to be.

Even so, I liked those evenings. I liked all of us together on that bed and Jess reading to us. After he died I found something he had written about that time.

"My Side of The Mountain *is the book that I used to try to hold my mother's and brother's and sister's lives together the summer we visited our mother. I had just read the book that spring, and by reading it to them in the evenings I wanted to create peace for us. It was my way of saying, 'Here we are together as a family again, finally. Mom, you have always wanted to provide me with the kind of care I need, and reading to you at bedtime is what I want to offer you. It is loving, restorative, calm, useful, and not contemplative or conjectural, and without the smell of death about it. I so well remember you reading to me. I loved best watching you read and being read to by you.'*

"So I recreated her act of care and I read to them in the evenings before bed. I enjoyed the story a second or third time myself. I read my little bible of reality to them, My Side of The Mountain, *a book about dirt and snow, seasons, rocks, and how to boil water in a leaf—physical realities.*

"*I had chosen this particular book because it told a great story about the attainment of independence, and because it was true. If there was anything the four of us needed by then it was truth. I read her the truth hoping against hope that she would reciprocate. I suspected my misplaced hope would lead to a dead end of some kind, but I never expected the literal dead end that was awaiting us at summer's end.*"

XI.

TIME PASSES SLOWLY ON MERCURY, THE SMALLEST PLANET, the one nearest the sun. They say one day there equals 176 of our earth days. Morning cartoons to lunch time to bedtime story and nearly half a year has passed back on planet earth.

We waited for long periods while she slept. I licked S&H Green Stamps at the kitchen table and carefully lined them up along the guidelines in the booklets, bringing order where I could. I pored over the catalogue imagining how I would spend the stamps, considering my options, weighing the baby doll with a trunk full of clothes against the toy oven, which came with real cake and brownie mixes. Each offered their various comforts.

The boys and I watched TV and slurped popsicles. We scratched bug bites, complaining of the heat. I read and played dolls. I counted my footsteps from bed to bath, from creek to backdoor. I told myself stories. I used the manual alphabet to talk to myself. I signed questions into my palm the way Helen Keller had done with Annie Sullivan. Down the hall in his room, Jess lay on the top bunk saying his name aloud over and over. He said he liked the sound of someone calling to him.

Jess was twelve that summer and took care of everything, or so it seemed to me. He was on top of things, he had the answer when I had a question. He told Toby and me jokes and made us brush our teeth. He organized the shows we put on and led our expeditions to the backyard creek. It would be a long time before I learned the price Jess was paying for his vigilance, for being the oldest and our champion and her shadow. In Austin, I only knew that he was near and I was better off for it, we all were.

Feeding us was hard for Mommy so Jess took over in the kitchen that summer. Mealtimes became extended elaborate performances staged not just for our nourishment but to appease the anxieties that the three of us shared. He colored placemats and wrote up menus with "The Brown Derby" scrawled across the front in a fancy script. He hung a paper napkin over his arm and escorted Toby and me with a flourish to the formica table in the kitchen for scrambled eggs and rice or instant potatoes and salad with Italian dressing.

In the living room he held sway at the piano. I had

lugged my practice books from New York but never sat down without prodding. Jess played, though. He played for us and for fun. He made things up, his fingers skipped, dancing. Sitting there, his back to us, he seemed in private negotiation with the instrument, calling forth what he required of it: Lively beat. Familiar tunes. He supplied the intermezzo while we waited for our lives to change, for childhood to conclude. He played as we tottered on the brink—unknowing but knowing just the same. I wished Mommy would take over for him, I wished she would sit at the piano like she used to. But she couldn't, so he had stepped up. He had been her understudy from the start. All his life he had been absorbing her secret message. He had taken it in with every breath: You and I, darling child, we are in this together. We will make it or not as a pair. There is no *me,* there is only *we.*

XII.

In july jess left for two weeks at friday mountain boys camp. He had been there the summer before and was eager to return. Mommy drove him up and we had barely passed through the main gate before he was bounding from the car, guitar case in hand, neither turning nor returning to say good-bye. I was surprised and hurt to have been so easily left and forgotten by our helmsman. I was anxious enough at his going. But he ran off without a backward glance, without expending whatever it would have cost him to prepare me for what was ahead. In any case he was free of it, and off like a shot, and his flight from that car was well-earned. Perhaps the final luxury of childhood.

Not long afterward I was woken up late at night by the sound of dishes and pots clanking in the kitchen. Mommy was in the bedroom doorway then. "Breakfast!" she said gaily. I lay unmoving, trying to work this through in my mind. She called then from the kitchen, "Right now, Laura! Before it gets cold."

I knew it was the middle of the night but I looked out the window to make sure. Black. Nighttime. On the stove was a pot of cooked oatmeal. She had made the whole carton, enough for twenty people or more. I sat down at the table, playing along, not knowing what else to do. She filled my bowl with hot cereal, far too hot for Texas in summer, even nighttime Texas. This was a winter meal, this was a New York winter breakfast. I nibbled at spoonfuls, wondering if she would wake Toby too, wondering if that would be better or worse. Every few bites she was beside me with another ladleful. The bowl was getting more full instead of less. This would never end. I put down my spoon, starting to cry.

"What is it?" she asked me. "You like oatmeal."

I hated this part. Cautiously then: "It's the middle of the night. And it's really hot. It's not time for breakfast."

"But we're *having* breakfast. It *is* time for breakfast. We're having breakfast. What's wrong with you?"

But it was too hot, it was too early, there was too much. And now she was mad at me. I had ruined it somehow, her offering. Toby came in then and she hollered at him to go back to bed right now and I hurried out after him.

I didn't blame her for wanting to rush nighttime. It was her worst time and I hated it too. She got trapped in her nightmares. Her fight was far away but the sounds of it reached across the distance to me. She ranged across the mattress, pleading. She whimpered and grabbed at my shoulder. I worked hard to wake her. It was an effort both merciful and self serving—I wanted her protection against the terror of the night.

She needed to be held and soothed. She needed comfort whispered down on her. She needed a more powerful sentinel than I to do battle for her, stronger arms than mine to lift her to her feet. I huddled on the sidelines in a tangle of sheets as she moaned and gritted her teeth like a woman bringing forth new life. But no new life was forthcoming. What was coming was death.

XIII.

WE SPENT AN EVENING AT THE DRIVE-IN. IT WAS A MOVIE we had seen and liked the winter before. I wanted Mommy to see it too. I knew she would like it and had told her all the best parts. She parked and we arranged pillows and snacks, each of us making an individual nest in the car and settling in for the show. I watched some of it but more often watched Mommy's face to gauge her enjoyment and to make certain she was giving the movie her undivided attention. I barely allowed her to blink or to fish in her purse for a match without a reprimand, "Watch this part, Mommy. This is good. Remember I told you about it? Watch." I wanted to give her this experience, something I had sampled and knew she would like. I had predigested it for her like a mama bird feeding its young.

The summer of 1966 was a time of unrest of all kinds, nationally and closer to home. Jess, returned from camp, was troubled and anxious by all that was happening and slept now with a kitchen knife under his bed pillow. That month of August both began and ended with death. On the first of the month, in what would come to be known as the "Texas Tower Massacre," a man named Charles Whitman climbed to the top of the tower of the university just before lunchtime. He had killed his mother and his wife the night before. And that next morning he packed sandwiches and a radio, six guns and some fruit cocktail, and settled in for an afternoon of murder. All told he would shoot forty-six people, killing fifteen, before police got to him and killed him.

As the news began to be reported, Mommy didn't seem afraid enough to suit me. I didn't know if she understood that what was happening was real and taking place nearby on campus. When Jess asked if we could go out to play, he was testing her. He knew that she would forbid it, that she must. But with her, "Sure, honey" she resoundingly flunked his test.

She failed the next one, too, though this was not one of our devising. It came of its own accord after dark. On an evening soon after the shootings the doorbell rang. She opened our door and looked down the staircase to the screen door below where a man stood. "Can I come on up? Is this it? How ya'll doin' tonight? Is this it?" He was loud and drunk and jolly. The sniper had been shot, they said so on TV, but who knew for sure? This guy could be anybody.

He could be a bad guy. Mommy didn't seem to sense any danger and acted as if she was about to let him in.

'Mommy, shut the door! Don't let him in. Mommy, don't go down." We grabbed at her robe and pulled her back from the door. Jess locked the door.

"But who is he? Maybe he needs something. Stop that! Who is he?"

"We don't know him, Mommy. He's a stranger. You can't let strangers in the house."

Dangers without and dangers within, and no one standing guard.

XIV.

We wanted Mommy happy, to feel loved, to feel at home on planet earth. We were careful of her feelings, always mindful of the collective power we had to send her spinning. We drew pictures for her and stirred up iced tea. We put on shows. We even staged a séance one evening. Our attempt, perhaps, to assure her a future the only way we could think of. I was to man the lights and Jess had assigned me two lines: "The séance has begun" and "the séance has ended." But I kept forgetting *séance,* an unfamiliar word—the diphthong did me in. 'Say-john', 'say-john' I kept muttering at my post beside the light switch. Jess read Mommy's future in an overturned Pyrex bowl, his flashlight shining underneath. He predicted health for her and another marriage. We watched her face for a reaction, eager to see whether he was promising what she wanted.

It would be how we would spend our summer, trying to guess the future she wanted so we could promise it to her.

But she was hard to read, languid. She thanked us in an amused but tired way, neither grateful nor ungrateful. She was elsewhere. Ebbing. Going through the motions, winding down. Going, going and almost gone. Did we sense it? Did that fuel our efforts to lure her back?

We tapped and sang, charmed and promised. We sold hard, giving it our all, selling her on life, on us, on the idea that it would be better than this, that it was worth it, that *we* were worth it. Frantically we danced. Did we know we were losing her? That we had already lost? Did we sense her withdrawal? Her hopelessness? Did we pick up somehow on a decision already made? We were racing against her clock, against a plan already in motion.

Socrates called children "the ties that bind a mother to life" and we clenched to our task in deadly earnest, circling her faster and tighter with our ties, binding her to us, to here, to now. We worked, shuffling and dancing around her, smiling, beguiling: Look! Look at us! Watch this! Stay! Here we are! We need you (sorry) but we're worth it. Stay, could you? Look what I can do, I can cook! I can cook my own meals! I can cook yours, too. I can read my own bedtime story! Wait, don't go. I can be what you need. What do you need? Who do you need me to be?

But she had found her poem and it was Shelley's—"How wonderful is Death, Death and his brother Sleep!"

Her response to us was unspoken but daily conveyed. Drained, apologetic: it isn't you, it's me. I can't. I do love you. Passionately. But it isn't enough. Maybe you'd be better off, anyway. I don't think you have what I need. And I know I don't have what you need. I'm not enough for you and you're not enough for me. You need me, I know. You want me, I feel that. But it's all just too much. Everyone knows what's best for me. Everyone knows what I should do. But let go, get off. Leave me alone. Get away. Step back. All of you. Just leave me alone. It's too noisy and it's too hard.

XV.

A COUSIN OF HERS, AN ART STUDENT AT THE UNIVERSITY, was painting her portrait that summer. Mommy went to sit for him weekly and reported on his progress. The portrait was to be life-size, she told us. *What does life-size mean? As big as a life? How big is a life?*

The sittings gave the two an opportunity to catch up and reminisce; both had grown up on Sunshine Ranch. They talked for hours. And although she sat unmoving in a corner of his studio, as her fears and memories and plans and pain were talked out, she began to take shape across the room on his canvas.

In the end she was blind. She said she was. I think the medication did something to her vision. She stopped driving and reading and admiring our artwork. We watched her eyes but they blinked as usual, she didn't look like the blind people on TV. And her sight seemed to come and go conveniently. When Toby stepped off a curb, she instantly snatched his arm. When I took a snack out of the fridge, she warned that it would spoil my dinner. "I thought you were blind," I crowed, victorious, but the look on her face prompted my instant regret.

Looking back through the checks she wrote that August it seems we went out almost daily. The checks written toward the end of the month are illegible, scrawled really. On August 17th she had the store fill in the check and she had only to sign her name. The first name is where it's supposed to be but the last name is broken into pieces and moves up and up with the middle *r* floating by itself above the other letters. She had the vacuum repaired on the 22nd and her hair done for nine dollars on the 25th. She wrote her last two checks, shakily, to Sommers drug store on the 25th and the 26th, my ninth birthday. Her last check cleared on the 31st, the day she died, leaving her $32.95 overdrawn.

I had my birthday on Friday and on Monday Big Laura came up from San Antonio to take us to the airport. And that's where we saw Mommy for the last time. When it was my turn to say good-bye, she was sitting and I was standing, so we were about the same height. I didn't pay enough attention to what she said. I didn't know how much it would matter.

That night she slept at Grandpa and Laura's, and the next day Mrs. Haslett gave her a ride to the airport for a short flight back up to Austin. "You love my children, Mathea," Mommy said to her. "Love them."

Mommy's body was found the next day by the cleaning lady. According to the police report, the doctor whose name was on the pill bottles by the bed was called and he "came to the scene. He stated he had prescribed sleeping pills to the victim." The coroner placed the death at nine that morning. It was August 31st and she was thirty-six.

We would never see her portrait, and it was never completed. Life-size indeed.

XVI.

WE DID NOT LEARN OF HER DEATH RIGHT AWAY. GRANDPA waited until the funeral and burial were past before letting Dad know. In the meantime we had arrived back in New York to spend a week with Dad in a temporary rental until our next house was available. Nick was home from school for a visit when we arrived, and Dad introduced all of us to Marcella, the new housekeeper.

The room I was directed to that first night was a tidy, ruffled haven and I loved it on sight. But I would come to resent the room its order and promise of sanctuary, a promise unfulfilled during my few nights in it. At school in the years afterward I would sometimes see the girl to whom that bedroom belonged, and I wanted to approach her. I wanted to tell her that my life had changed at her house one day while she was away at the seashore. I wanted to tell her I had cried in her bed. But I knew her only by sight. And our link was an inexpressible one.

On Saturday morning, Dad came into the kitchen in his robe as I was finishing my breakfast. He looked miserable and had a white mustache from the ulcer medicine he sometimes swigged.

"You look awful," I informed him.

"Well, I didn't get very much sleep last night," he snapped, though he seemed instantly to regret it and patted my shoulder as he walked back out of the room.

I was eager for the boys to get up. We had planned a walk to town that morning. We had never lived near enough the village to walk, and I was excited at the prospect of going into town unaccompanied.

But as soon as the boys were up and had eaten, Dad herded all of us into the living room, even Marcella. And this is my first real memory of her: wiping her hands on a dishtowel as she came into the living room looking solemn. She and Dad didn't look at one another and I could tell somebody was in trouble. She sat down next to me.

I was chewing gum as I sat down, something Dad didn't like us to do. As I reached my hand up to sneak it out of my mouth, I glanced over at Marcella to see if she was watching. She was, but there was no reproach in her look. She smiled a small smile and we became friends in that instant before my life changed.

Dad raised his left arm and put it around my shoulders

and squeezed too hard just as he began to speak. I was crunched up against him, uncomfortable and wanting to push away, but I didn't. I knew enough to sit still and listen. His words were confusing, though.

"Children, on Tuesday night Mommy went to sleep and never woke up."

What does that mean? There was a blink of time in which nothing happened at all. We balanced on an instant in silence, balanced between understanding what he meant and not. Jess got it. It shot from his ear to his brain to his heart to his mouth and it came out in a cry. And that is the sound that tipped me over into knowing. Jess translated for us as he had done so often before. He rendered the news. He brought it to us, and we cried.

XVII.

IT SEEMED AN ENDLESS TIME BEFORE DAD SPOKE AGAIN. He could only tell us as much as he had been told, which was little. Her overdose had not yet been conceded by anyone in Texas, so even Dad did not yet know with certainty. And yet he did know. And so did we. Nevertheless, he tried hard to steer us elsewhere. He spoke vaguely of a brain tumor, a sudden illness.

We talked that day but not as we needed to, not honestly. We spoke as we were able, in the tip-toeing, side-stepping dance we had been trained in from the start. And by the time we all stood up, life resumed. Marcella returned to the kitchen and Dad went to shower and we children took our walk to town. And Mommy had been placed on a high shelf and out of our reach. We children would be quick to grasp the unspoken imperative that she was not to be mentioned. Much as we would long to talk about her, we would not be brave enough against Dad's pain and the huge expanse of silence surrounding her.

In bed that night I cried, careful to be quiet. But Dad came in a bit later and pulled me onto his lap, and we cried some more. I marveled at his appearing just when I most needed him and wondered how he knew.

In the days afterward there would be neither flowers nor visitors nor references to Mommy's death made in our presence. She had been gone from New York for two years, she and Dad were divorced, and the circumstances of her death were unknown and only assumed. No one knew what to say and so nothing was said.

There is a finality in death, and yet so much now began silently working and twisting and tangling inside each one of us. She had always needed us as much as we had needed her. What would she do now without us? And what of us? Her embrace was our home place. What were we to do without her? Her pain had always been our pain, her fears shared by us all. What were we now to do with the weight of all that? She had found it unbearable. Could we carry it for her? Should we carry on, or no? When Mommy declared, "I am not worthy of life," the worth of each of her children was called into question. Her death lit death fires in each of us.

Jess in particular would never stray far from that day's

loss or from any of the losses of Mommy that preceded that final one. He was twelve now and by this time his life already was set on a course that would later horrify in its seeming inevitability.

If, as Millay says, childhood is the kingdom where nobody dies, we were banished from the kingdom that day. A huddled few moments on a stranger's couch removed our mother from our lives. But our loss of her already had crept across several years, claiming more and more of our hope and comfort in small snatches as Mommy, in one way or another, had come to be absent from us. Those minutes on that couch only served to place the final dot on a sentence that we already knew by heart.

The Decree of Endless Silence

I.

NICK RETURNED TO SCHOOL A DAY OR TWO LATER AND the rest of us moved to the next house. This one was the small gatehouse of an old estate. Toby and I shared one bedroom and Jess was in the other. Dad slept in the dining room and Marcella was in a little utility room off the kitchen.

Marcella moved us through those months, those first months. Guidelines were erected and patrolled. *You are not to speak that way, sit that way, reach across the table.* She was in the car, in the kitchen, over the homework. I watched her cook and started to learn. I watched her quilt and wanted to try. Dad was often out in the evenings so if I came down in the night looking for comfort, I headed through the kitchen to Marcella's room. We sat on her bed and talked. I liked looking at the family pictures of her children, now grown. We had to speak quietly, which only made our night-time talks more secret and special.

Marcella needed nothing from me. I had in her a place to rest. I sometimes sought her counsel about Barbara, whom Dad was seeing. They had been dating since the week Mommy died. Barbara came over for dinner or out with us on weekends, and we were straining to make a connection. We all tried hard, too hard, to have fun together and to bridge what was a great divide. The only thing we had in common was Dad.

We were emotional and expressive and eager for attention and affection, even Dad. She was cerebral and brisk, a successful businesswoman to whom displays of affection or emotion were unnerving. She was lean in both form and manner. Tall, she seemed to look down on us from her height. Time after time I would dash up, eager and open, only to be stiff- armed. It felt as if every approach met with nettle and bramble. "The fact is, Laura, . . ." she would intone, and my spirits would sink even before hearing whatever pronouncement would follow. Even the sound of my own name seemed to chill in her mouth.

The wedding was on April Fool's Day, seven months after Mommy's death. At the reception a family friend, drunk, cornered me for an urgent whispered conference. "What did you call your mother?" she demanded. Embarrassed, but without the nerve to lie to a grownup, I admitted the truth: "Mommy."

"Well, then call Barbara something else, 'Mom' or something, OK?"

"OK."

"And listen—get that middle piece of wedding cake. It holds the best luck."

"OK."

I hung around the cake table, and when the cake was cut the treasured piece was mine at last. I took it outside and stopped to eat it under a flowering cherry tree in Barbara's front yard. But I had been making the rounds of the candy dishes all afternoon and the first bite of cake threatened to make me sick. I dropped it without ceremony into dead leaves and mulch.

II.

After the wedding there was a move to another house, another neighborhood, another school, my fourth in five years. Marcella was let go and replaced by posters of house rules taped to kitchen walls. There were smaller signs on the telephones and bathroom mirrors. We hesitated to take a step or to ask a question, there was a lot to remember. Toby dried himself off with the bathmat once because he didn't know if we were allowed to take towels out of the linen closet.

Nick was brought home at Dad's insistence but was allowed to stay only long enough to raise his hopes and to taste that unaccustomed word, *home.* He was eleven now, almost twelve, and his visits home always were hard on him. He wanted so much to be one of us again. But we children were discouraged from "congregating," a new word to me, or even talking too much to one another. If two of us were in a room, and a third one came in, one of us was expected to leave. That was the rule. We were encouraged to keep busy and not to dwell on or talk about the past. There were no photographs of Mommy in the house. The silence and blank space around her stretched out in every direction.

Jess's first suicide attempt came six months after the wedding. I was brushing my teeth one early morning when I saw Dad out the window running to his car with something large in his arms wrapped in a blanket.

"Jess has pneumonia." Barbara told us at breakfast. Behind her we could see that the doorframe to his bedroom was splintered. Dad had had to break in to get to Jess.

Later in the day Dad and Barbara appeared in the doorway of my fifth-grade classroom and my teacher excused me to go out to them in the hallway. Dad smiled and gripped my forearms too hard saying with insistence, "Jess is OK. He's going to be OK." The urgency in his voice and the look on his face frightened me in a new way.

A few evenings later Toby asked Dad if he could send his Halloween candy to Jess at the hospital, and Dad started to cry. In small ways, unspoken ways, we came to know that this was bad, something worse than pneumonia, something that could not even be uttered.

Weeks passed. *Can we visit? Can we call?* No, honey. He'll be home soon. It's better to just let him rest. *Rest. He's gone for a rest, like Mommy used to do.*

When Jess did come home from the hospital, I wonder what Dad said to keep him from making reference to his suicide attempt. I wonder if he told Jess that they had kept it from Toby and me and not to mention it. And I can imagine Jess's reply, always apologetic and eager to please, "Oh, OK. Sure. I can do that, I understand. Sorry for the bother, really." He was back in our midst, but already at fourteen Jess and his pain had become as unspeakable as Mommy was.

On that first Christmas Eve together as a new family, we sang carols around the tree. We sang "The First Nöel." And with what sadness and anger and defiance I sang Mommy's name into that house.

III.

Perhaps a year after the wedding Marcella reappeared. She was in need of a job and was rehired, to my great happiness. She was settled into another small room off another kitchen and I began again to find my late-night way to the sanctuary of her room by the light of the kitchen stove clock.

There was not yet an ease between Barbara and me. Our exchanges were stiff and awkward and it seemed to take every ounce of her patience to tolerate children with sad faces. I continued to turn to Marcella for comfort and advice. Dad caught me sneaking down the stairs to her room a time or two, and he asked me to stop going to her. He and Barbara also asked Aunt Peggy and Ann, a friend of Mommy's, to stop phoning or coming to see us. The hope was that by removing familiar comforts we children would turn more naturally and easily to Barbara.

Another December and Marcella was let go once again.

Barbara came to my room one evening to let me know that Marcella would be leaving the next day and I was free to go down to say good-bye if I would like to.

I took her Christmas gift from my closet and went down to leave it at her bedroom door. It was something I had made for her in art class at school, hers was the first and only gift I had prepared. As I passed back through the kitchen, Marcella was there and smiled at me. "Thank you, Laura," she said but, crying hard, I could only nod.

Throughout the next school day I berated myself for my silence and thought about all that I should have said, and planned what I would say when I got home. But of course she was gone by then. And I would have no more word of her for almost thirty years.

Four months later it was Dad who came to my room on another evening to tell me that a Texas visit had been arranged for me. *A visit to Texas? Wonderful. When?*

"Day after tomorrow. You're due for a tetanus shot and you can go by school tomorrow to empty your locker and hand in your books and say good-bye to your friends and you leave the next morning."

"But it's the middle of school. Why would I empty my locker? What about school?"

"They have schools in Texas, don't they?"

But if it's only a visit why would I go to school there? How

long is this for? Is this punishment or prize? Blessing or banish-
ment? Am I to be grateful or guilty? Happy or sad?

When Dad had first called Big Laura, I later learned, and asked if she would take me, she had said no. And when he asked again, she had said no again. She was just getting back on her feet after breast cancer surgery and a year of chemo and cobalt treatments. And Grandpa had left her. When the cancer diagnosis had come in, he had walked out. For Laura it was the weakest of times physically and emotionally, and she did not feel up to caring for anyone. But Dad kept up the calls—he and Barbara believed this would be best—and, worn down, Laura ultimately gave in.

IV.

As I walked through the back door into Laura's den that first night, two things caught my eye—a large glass jar filled with colorful candies, and Laura's graceful maple rocking chair, which I remembered from years before. And there can be no more fitting emblems to represent the years I would spend in Big Laura's house. I could not yet know it, but there were ahead of me hundreds of days and nights of sweetness and color and comfort. There would soon be for us both the soothing rhythm of routine and the comfort of kindred hearts. Big Laura and Little Laura would find their consolation together.

It was wonderful to be with her again and I didn't want to let her out of my sight. I was happy to return to that familiar house, to be back in Texas where Mommy was known and loved and came up so naturally in conversation. "Your mama," Laura called her. "Your mama loved you children more than anything in the world." "Your mama was a stunningly beautiful woman." "Your poor mama just had a real hard time with things."

Laura and I easily fell into a shared home life. As I was, she was a creature of habit and I had only to know the day of the week to know what I could expect for breakfast, lunch or dinner. She joked that she was the only person she knew who had to dust her stove top, so little was it used. Instead we went out or brought food in. Several nights a week we went to Luby's, the local cafeteria, and on Wednesdays we picked up fried chicken on my way home from ballet class. I was a round but earnest ballerina.

We shared a tendency to be exacting, to talk too much, to get the giggles. We developed the private jokes and traditions and code words that any couple accrues over time. I had never heard of a mutual admiration society until I heard her describe us that way to a friend. She had a weakness for garage sales and ice cream shops and we rarely passed either one without stopping with a squeal of her brakes and a squeal of her own. I was quick to discover in her a quality I prized but had never encountered in a grown-up—Big Laura had a sweet tooth to rival my own.

Classmates assumed she was my mother, and I never bothered to correct them. I would not have known how. There was no easy way to characterize our connection and we laughed about that. She was my ex-step-grandmother to be exact. But I was her child. She called me her spiritual child. I moved into her home and into her life and she laid claim to me with a firm, sure, generous grip. Neither flesh of her flesh nor bone of her bone, but hers in a wonderful way.

Soon after my arrival she opened a dresser drawer and showed me her ribs. She had had tuberculosis in her twenties and ever since then had kept the ribs that had been removed to collapse her lung. I was enrolled in sixth grade at the local elementary school and asked to take the ribs with me to science class one day. But that morning I moved too quickly as I was getting out of the car and dropped the box. I was mortified as scattering, clattering bones skidded across the sidewalk. And as I leapt from the car to retrieve them, Big Laura, shrieking with laughter, yelled from the driver's seat in mock outrage, "Is *that* any way to treat your grandmother?!"

V.

SHE WAS MY AUNTIE MAME, BUT WITH A WONDERFUL weighty side. One evening she tossed me a matchbook and asked me to light some candles on the table. A few minutes later when she passed back through I was still standing there and had to tell her, embarrassed, that I couldn't light a match. I was afraid of fire and getting burned.

The next morning as I was finishing breakfast she sat down beside me and slid a box of matches over toward my plate. "Today you're going to light one match for me," she said. "Just one, honey."

"No, I'm not!" I said, horrified. "I can't. And I don't want to." When she insisted, I used every argument that came to mind. I wheedled. I joked. "I'll never smoke cigarettes if I can't light a match!" And finally, when I saw that she would not be dissuaded, I cried.

"You have to do this," she said to me. "Look how much power fear has over you! Do not allow yourself to be so shaky and limited. It limits how God can use you. Don't you limit the Lord, Laura!" It was a favorite phrase of hers, I was to discover. "You light me one match and we'll blow it right out and get on with our day."

I made several attempts that day before I finally succeeded, tearful and fearful. I made her move with me over to the kitchen sink and fill it with water before I would try. And the next day she was back again at the kitchen table with her box of matches. This was an assignment I would face every morning for months. I did not leave for school until I had taken my vitamins, brushed my teeth and lit a match. If I was going to sleep at a friend's house I had to light tomorrow's match before leaving home. I learned to strike a match fearlessly, unthinkingly.

Years later, when I was fifteen, I made a large cross for Laura for Christmas. I copied a piece of Mexican folk art I had seen. Glued in an intricate pattern on a large cardboard cross were 238 burned wooden matches. It had a wonderful look and smell to it, and for twenty years until she died it would sit on Laura's mantle as silent testimony to triumphs large and small in both of our lives. I was never more excited or proud to present a gift to anyone as I was that Christmas. As Laura opened the package I knew just what she would say when she saw the gift, and she did not disappoint me. "What a victory for the Lord."

God was a friend of Big Laura's. She talked to Him and about Him throughout the day. I had never known anyone to be on such friendly and casual terms with God. She included Him in every decision and unceasingly sent up prayers over the smallest concerns of our lives. She prayed with me and for me. She prayed her beloved oak tree at the ranch through a seven-year drought in the fifties and an outbreak of oak wilt decades later. She would pray me through math tests, ballet recitals and, in time, child-birth. Good news, cancer news, snake bite, IRS audit. Her life of challenges, her life of celebrations, was a life of prayer.

VI.

Big Laura had a tendency to be single-minded, to devote herself fully to the topic or project at hand, and for twenty-six months I was her willing and grateful project. She helped with homework and enthusiastically took over my school reports. She gave me her time, she answered my questions. It was she who told me the truth about Jess's suicide attempt. It came up as naturally in conversation between us as it seemed everything else did. Soon after I arrived she told me she would take me out to my mother's grave. She thought it was important, and I wondered how she knew how much I had wanted to go.

We went after school one day. It was three years by now since Mommy had died. On the long drive to the cemetery Laura told me again about the sculpture I would see at Mommy's grave. Grandpa's cousin Mary had made it. "You children were the most precious thing to your mama and Grandpa thought it seemed just right to have your faces there on that stone," she said.

Just outside the cemetery gates we stopped to buy flowers, and I chose a little pot of yellow mums. Once in the park, we had not driven far when suddenly there it was. I could see it from the car even before we stopped and got out. There were Toby and me and Nick and Jess. Coming closer, I could read Mommy's name and the dates at the bottom. When Laura brushed at the leaves and twigs on top of the stone, I knew I was allowed to touch it too. I ran my fingers over our faces.

"Her middle name was Flowers?" I asked her.

"Mm-hmm. A family name, I think."

Laura kept up light conversation. She probably worried that being here would be upsetting to me but I didn't feel sad. I was grateful to be here. I had wanted to be.

To the left of Mommy's grave was Ada Lee's, the grandmother I had never known. Several years in the future Jess would be on the right. I stood there and read Ada Lee's tombstone while Laura watched me and waited, smiling.

"Is that Grandpa?" I asked, and she laughed.

"That's him!"

When his first wife had died, Grandpa had erected a

tombstone for them both, so her stone included his name and birth date. All that was missing was the date of his death.

"He wanted to make sure he would be buried next to her," Laura explained. "He used to bring me out here and we would clean things up and leave flowers. I used to ask him, 'So, where are you planning to put me, at your feet?' But he didn't laugh. He never did give me an answer either, come to think of it."

We were in the family section of the cemetery, which spread out over a large area. Colorful kin in every direction and Laura led me from stone to stone supplying a running commentary on who was whose mother or cousin or child, and where I fit in, exactly how I was linked to every one of them. She gave me the stories, the family history, the connections. Riches.

VII.

OUR EVERY DAY BEGAN THE SAME WAY. "UP AND AT 'EM, Madam. It's time to get up!" On her way to the kitchen to get my breakfast, Laura would call into my room. Later, if I happened into her room as she was dressing, I would step up behind her to rub my fingers down the length of her scars. Hundred of stitches from the tuberculosis and breast cancer formed long tracks like a zipper down her back and under her right arm. I could reach where she could not, and she was always grateful to have them rubbed. It eased the tightness and itch, she said.

Every Friday after school we packed her car and left town for the weekend. Laura's family had been ranching sheep in the hill country north of town for nearly a century. The land there was hilly and covered with cedar and live oak trees, nothing like south Texas or Grandpa's cattle ranches.

Laura's sister Dottie was always at the ranch on weekends too. Her house was near Laura's and we would spend much of the weekend there. Dottie's house was a fun place to be and much more lively than ours. It was always full of people, her three children and all the family and friends who appeared, expected or unexpected, for the weekend or afternoon. The open stone hearth at Dottie's was the gathering spot for anyone who happened to be in the area as the sun was going down. I sat there month after month taking in the stories and reminiscences and tall tales. In cooler months the fire was kept going all evening, but year-round the talk and laughter lasted all weekend.

How different it was from Dad's house. The kindling in his fireplace back in New York tended to be tensely wadded pages of the *New York Times*. And those fires were admired through perfectly fitted glass doors, doors that cut us off from the warmth of the fire and the pop and life of the flames. Still, it was home. And fun as Texas was to me, much as I felt loved and wanted there, it was never entirely my world. However long it lasted, it was always just a visit. And I was always a visitor.

I didn't know how long the visit to Texas would last. I didn't know that Dad called Laura periodically and asked her to keep me a few more months. Laura believed I more rightly belonged with Dad, and she didn't hesitate to tell him so. But by then we had made a happy life together and she was willing to have me stay.

In August, during the peak of meteor showers, Dottie would organize a campout in the pasture every year. "Camp Shooting Star" she called it. Whoever was around came along. Laura brought over her rollaway bed in the back of the pickup, and the rest of us brought the sleeping bags and ice chests, marshmallows and guitars.

We would watch the night sky for hours entirely undisturbed by city lights or noise. We would lie there talking and singing and exclaiming in unison at every streak across the summer sky. Homesick as I was at times, and much as I missed Dad, every shooting star I saw and every moment of that late-night laughter were proof to me of a loving God and of the magic of my motherland.

VIII.

Dear Barbara and Gil,

I wanted you to know Laura's reaction when I told her that she would spend the winter here with me. She just sat still and seemed quite stunned. I think she was really counting on going back home for good at that point and was deeply disappointed, and rightly or wrongly she felt quite rejected by you both. Her reaction sort of stunned me. I know that she wishes she were two Lauras so that she could stay here and be there too. But I think she is beginning to know who she is and where she belongs and what I would like to ask of you is this—please be very sure that Laura's return to me is the best solution for all concerned. Please keep an open mind and an open heart while she is at home on this visit. I know that it is difficult at times to read a situation correctly, but I do know that Laura wants desperately to belong somewhere and to have a home and family to which she really belongs. She hasn't ever really felt that in her life evidently, and it is difficult for her to put down roots here as she knows this is not a permanent situation either.

I just thought that you should know the reaction that I got. I guess that is all for now, but maybe another chat is in order now.

Love,

Laura

P.S. The thing or thought that keeps coming to my mind, and I'm going to throw it out for what it's worth, I feel very strongly that Laura has now "outgrown" me, that is, she needs more people around her—brothers and sisters and a man around the house, a father, (and a mother!)

NOVEMBER 1969

Dear Barbara and Gil,

I'm glad that you made the reservation for Laura to come home for Christmas, because I think she will want to be with her family then. Bless her heart, again she wishes she could be in two places at once, but I think she has about decided to go home for Christmas. I have told her that it is her decision and not mine, and however she decides is fine with me. I'd love to have her here, but I'd also love for her to be with you, where she belongs. She feels that there is too long a time to go without seeing you if she doesn't go home for Christmas. June seems a long way off to her. I personally think it might be best for her to 'touch home base' again now, but I don't have any intention of putting any pressure on her one way or another. She has been rather nostalgic about home lately and she wants to see all of you and she's anxious to meet the new puppies, etc.

I must dash. It's my car-pool day again, but I wanted to get this letter off to you about the Christmas holidays. Let us hear from you.

Love,
Laura

FEBRUARY 1970

Dear Barbara and Gil,

I am happy to report that Laura is fine again — her

scratched-up back is practically healed and the head injury is proving to be a minor one. I had the doctor check her thoroughly again on Thursday. He wants her to refrain from any type of exertion for another week or ten days. So we are doing exactly as he orders (which isn't always easy as Laura is her usual bouncy happy self again now.) I do think it will be a while before we get her back on a horse.

As for Laura's coming back to me for the school year next year, we do need to talk about that. Yes, she is happy here, but she does belong at home with her family and I think she has healed enough now to do fine there, particularly if she feels wanted. Rightly or wrongly, she hasn't felt really and truly wanted. I know differently, of course, but she must know it, and that is up to you and Barbara. I love having Laura here. She is a delight to me, but the question of where Laura should be next year goes beyond what I want or what Laura wants or what you and Barbara want. And that is what will have to be decided.

But enough. I've got to dash. Let us hear from you.

With love to all,

Laura

NOVEMBER 1970

Dear Gil,

I had intended to write before now, but as you know, time has a way of flying by and getting away from us.

Laura and I have been ailing, not seriously, just some bug that hasn't really gotten us down for long. But we haven't felt like running any footraces lately. We hope to spend Thanksgiving in the Hill Country — we will either go up there on Wednesday, after school or Thursday morning. Depends on how we feel. Then we will stay there until Sunday. All of my family will be up there and it will be a happy time for us all.

Laura is doing fine — she was so thrilled with her report card — we were both so proud of her. She has such a full life — many friends — and is learning to know herself and to really like herself. She sings and dances around the house all the time and is a happy person most of the time. Sometimes she gets 'blue,' but not for long. She speaks of all of you often and with love.

There is always something going on, it seems, and we would welcome another 4 or 5 hours each day so we could squeeze it all in.

I hope you all have a happy Thanksgiving. Let us hear from you.

My love to all,

Laura

IX.

AFTER EIGHT GRADE, WHEN SCHOOL LET OUT FOR SUM-
mer, I left Texas and returned to Dad's house and New
York. It was time for high school, a good time to make the
move.

I was home ten days before I found myself on a train
bound for a two-month summer camp in upstate New
York. In August, days before my fourteenth birthday and
the start of high school I returned to Dad's house.

Going from Texas back to Dad's was in some ways a
step from firm ground back down into sand. Laura's house
meant open arms, honest talk, love notes on my pillow, in
my book bag, hidden in the toe of my ballet slipper: "You
are my beloved spiritual child and that will never change.
Always remember that, dear one." "I know that God is in
control of your life. You are in His tender care always and
in all ways." "Bless your heart, you made my bed! You are
a dear girl and I love you." I belonged in the passenger seat

of Big Laura's Jeep. I belonged in the middle bedroom at the center of her house. I belonged on her right at the breakfast table. She always introduced me not by name but by relationship. "This is Noël's child" or "Rowena's niece," or "Jess's granddaughter."

Back at Dad's house it was less clear to me where I belonged, or who or whose I was. At Dad's house I was just Laura. And there was little sense of connection or relatedness between any of us in that house. Dad and Barbara kept to their heavy work schedules. Only Eve, the quiet housekeeper, was always home. I would find her sitting on a kitchen stool looking out the window at the green of the trees. She had left her children far away in Jamaica to cook for us and clean our house. She slept in the attic bedroom that once had been mine. Almost all of them had been mine. Almost all of them had been all of ours. We moved from room to room without tie or root.

As school was starting, I wondered if clothes and interests would be the same as they had been among my friends in Texas. I wondered if I would fit in. I did not yet know that I was beginning high school with a terrific distinction. It turned out I was far more than just Laura. I was Jess Gordon's little sister. He was a senior that year and I was a freshman. And I was about to rediscover that being Jess's sister counted for something wonderful.

It seemed that only I, who had been away so long, was unaware of Jess's status among our peers. Everyone knew Jess. In an era of greasers and jocks and preppies, he was cool by anyone's measure, greeted by name as he idled down the hallways or rifled vaguely through his locker for the term paper he was pretty sure was in there somewhere. He featured prominently in school plays and talent shows. He gave concerts to raise money for student causes. At school he was a folk hero of sorts with his crumpled clothes and hiking boots, admired for his music, his wit, his poet's heart. Jess, who shared a birthday with T.S. Eliot and George Gershwin and Johnny Appleseed.

X.

Y OU WOULDN'T FIND JESS IN THE LIBRARY DOING RESEARCH or preparing for an exam. He likely didn't even know it was exam week. But you might find him in a study carrel sneaking a nap. You wouldn't find him in the gym. He wasn't on any sports teams. But you might find him back behind the gym tossing a ball to somebody's dog or playing his banjo or rolling a joint. If you came late to school you might see him racing into the school parking lot on his Schwinn. He wouldn't be sitting on the seat, though. His feet would be up on the seat and he would be down in a tight crouch, his hair flying out behind him, his eyes in a squint against the wind.

As a senior, facing decisions about college and moving on and growing up, Jess grew increasingly anxious and despondent. His class voted him "Most Disorganized" that year and everyone chuckled. It fit. But he was worried, he was grieving. His outer state reflected the inner chaos, and as it intensified his reputation at school became even more entrenched, adding to the burden. The nearer he came to falling apart, the harder everyone laughed.

He was cheered for his distractedness, for his lame excuses in math class. It was expected that he would not have his homework, that he would have left the science project on the bus or under a tree. His vague answers had teachers shaking their heads in resigned amusement and the other kids grinning and slapping each other in high-fives. He was in a deadly slide that everyone took to be the enviable cool of one laid-back guy.

He was reading Hotchner's biography of Hemingway that year. I used to see it open on his bedside table. Was he seeking a role model as a man, as a writer, or as someone suicidally depressed? Who knew. No one was talking at our house.

It was lonely living there. Each of us occupied our solitary track, and rarely did they touch or converge. There was no air of camaraderie in the family, of rooting for one another, no sharing of confidences or thoughts or burdens. Most of us only shared tension and anxiety and a sense that we were doing it all wrong, whatever it was.

Barbara chided Jess for having a depressive influence on the household and for being morose, a new word to me.

Early in the school year he was asked to move out and he went to live with family friends across town.

After that it was easier for Jess and me to spend time together. We could meet freely at school. We talked more in his last months of high school than we had in years. We talked about things at home, about missing Dad, who always seemed to be angry. The past called to us too, and we would find our circumspect conversations heading back in time. It was not morbidity that drew us into reminiscences about Mommy and Doe Hill. It was not that Jess and I had nothing else to talk about. Neither was it self-pity or a way to exclude Barbara, though she thought it was. It was just that there was so much unspoken, unfinished, and our hearts felt the weight of it.

XI.

Both Jess and I had chorus during first period with Mr. Dunn, and so every school day began with singing together. We spent that year learning the Brahms Requiem, among other pieces. I have never forgotten the words, and I wonder if they were as soothing to Jess that year as they were to me. *Blessed are they that mourn for they shall have comfort. Yea, I will comfort you, as one whom his own mother comforteth. He that sows in tears shall reap in joy. Ye know that for a little time labor and sorrow were mine, but at the last I have found comfort. Joy and gladness, these shall be their portion. And pain and sighing shall flee from them.*

After school Jess and I spent time together in the foreign language lab. We were required to spend a certain number of hours each week listening to language tapes, and I'm sure Jess's presence in the lab was always noted with surprise and approval by the teacher on duty; we signed in together often. But the tapes we spooled onto the reel-to-reel machines were neither my Spanish dialogues nor his French conversation tapes. They were the tapes I had lifted from a box in the back of Dad's closet and had sneaked out of the house in the bottom of my book bag. They were the old tapes from Doe Hill.

The two of us squeezed into a study carrel meant for one. Our heads would be so close together that our huge padded headphones nearly touched as we tuned into life at our old house. There were bits we knew by heart but they still made us laugh. Toby at age five or so learning to read, my bossing everyone around, somebody's missed cue when we sang, the general hilarity and hysteria, and Dad yelling for all of us to just pipe down.

We could anticipate when each screech was coming, an angry voice too close to the mike or somebody's Christmas morning tantrum, and Jess or I would make a grab for the volume knob to save our ears. We would get to laughing so hard at the insanity of it all that we would have to put our heads down on the desk to keep the teacher from coming over to investigate.

Once in a great while, too rarely, Mommy's voice was heard among the rabble. Never loudly enough and never for long. But on hearing her, our grins would fade to smaller, more cautious smiles and we would freeze, afraid to miss a sound. We would turn our heads apart slightly, respectful of each other's privacy in those moments. When her voice ended, one of us might reach up to rewind the tape a second or two and we would lean in, voracious, eyes shut to hear better. "Look, Lolly, at your new doll. Isn't she darling?" *It was real. That was her. I just heard her. She had been there with us. And happy. There was delight in her voice.*

"I don't remember her calling me *Lolly,*" I'd say to Jess.

"She called you that a lot. And she usually called Nicky 'Nicholas'."

"I love to hear her sing. I wish there was more of her singing."

XII.

As my classmates were venturing out in small ways and beginning to make the break from their mothers, I still sought mine. I was trying to discover who she was and thereby who I was in a house where she was never mentioned. I studied the few photographs of her that I had accumulated in Texas. I studied her face with more interest than I did my own.

When Jess left for college, I stopped taking tapes to school. I began to seek out Mommy's voice in other ways. At home I made my way down the length of our living room bookshelves looking for books with her name in them. There were not many. Most of her things had gone with her to Texas at the time of the divorce. But there were a few, and when I found one I took it up to my room.

Her books tended to be heavily marked up, and I would study the underlined portions attempting to divine her interest. I was trying to get to know her, to infer her thoughts based on what she had starred in pencil. Sometimes whole pages were underlined and I would make my way slowly through, trying to guess what it all had meant to her. She favored poetry. Seven of Emily Dickinson's poems were starred, six about death and one about hope. That seemed to be Mommy's life recipe—six parts death to one part hope. In her own poetry, death was always a friend, something lovely and warm. As I made my way through her books, if I came across a piece of the puzzle I couldn't fit in or didn't like the looks of, I simply ignored it. I reconstructed her and constructed myself out of whatever remained.

In early childhood all of my senses and reactions and many of my thoughts had been attuned to Mommy, and many remained now in her service. I had been her lifelong student trying to understand her, to know her as my source. In adolescence and early adulthood she was my frame of reference. My sense of who I was remained rooted in who she was. I was her offshoot, her offspring, her lesser branch. I tried haltingly to recreate her, guessing at half of it. Trying to be her was a way of keeping her with me. And it nicely filled in the empty holes where my own identity should have been but was not yet.

I tended to focus on all the ways that I was not her. Hers was the face I sought when I did look in the mirror. I imagined that everyone who had loved her was measuring me, searching my face and manner for someone else but finding, regrettably, only me. I didn't have her dark hair, her beauty, her smile, her singing voice. I was failing everyone who missed Mommy, and I was chief among them. I cut my nails short and grew my hair long. I practiced her handwriting. I pored over her books. I took my cues from her however I could get them. I started smoking her brand of cigarettes at fourteen. I started sneaking sleeping pills and tranquilizers from Dad's closet—Jess told me where to find them. I drank, though I hated both the taste and the effects. I was up against the example Mommy had set before me in her life and in her death. Rejecting any of it felt wasteful. There was so little of her to spare.

XIII.

BLANK FACES AROUND OUR DINNER TABLE. HALTING ATtempts at conversation. Dad leapt up in the middle of one meal to demonstrate the Heimlich maneuver, which he had learned that day at work. *Would it only work on food?* I wondered, watching him. *What would it take to bring up all the unspoken, disallowed words lodged in my throat?* I was fifteen and could barely speak to anyone without tears pooling and leaking out of my averted eyes.

Dad knew how unhappy I was and asked once or twice if I thought living with another family would help. *But is that our only option? Couldn't I stay home and be welcome? Can't that be one of our choices?*

Maybe not. Because when every intention is to outrun memory and guilt, tears like mine and pain like Jess's were worse than inconvenient. They were accusation and daily indictment. The slate has been wiped clean, a new reality hastily constructed. And sad faces messed with the program, the plan, the new plan. Snap out of it, kids, this is a new day, we're going to get it right this time. With another big house, another pool, another wife and pair of dogs and cool car for Dad.

I did want to keep my place at the family table. So I kept quiet. I had learned the lessons of the house. Show your pain and be shown the door. Shout into the silence and find yourself on a plane or a train headed somewhere far away. Nick's removal, my time in Texas, Jess's banishment, had not been lost on me. I would do what was necessary to be allowed to stay. I would joke. I would entertain. I would amuse. And when I could not, I would keep to my room and listen to Judy Garland records.

Garland's rich voice, her desperation, reminded me of Mommy. Last thing every night I played the final seconds of her 1960 Carnegie Hall concert on the record player by my bed. After the singing, after all the encores, while everyone was still clapping and cheering, she called out to the thousands (but really only to me), "Goodnight! I love you very much. Good night! God bless."

I did not sleep well, and never enough. Invariably the passing school bus I had just missed was the sound that wakened me to another day. I rose reluctantly, exhausted, late again. I cried as I dressed. I cried as I walked to school. I would have been up well past midnight the night before, delaying lights-out as long as possible and that dreadful silence.

When it was quiet, questions came to mind and pain came to heart. I lay there in my bed, in Mommy's bed. The four-poster had been shipped up to me after she died as something to remember her by. I remembered the bed. We had shared it that summer in Austin. It was where she had had her nightmares and I had urgently, fearfully, shaken her awake. Night after night she would go to sleep and I would wake her up. That was our routine. And she had played her part and I had played my part right up until the end. Until that night when she was there, and I was not.

XIV.

I ASKED DAD IF I COULD GO INTO A HOSPITAL. ODD REQUEST for a child. He patted my hand and said no, that was not the answer. But he never said what was.

What did a psychiatric hospital mean to me as a young teenager? What was I hoping to find there? I had never been inside one. My friends with problems at home were going off to boarding school. Why not that? What did I seek in asking to go to a hospital?

It seemed to me it would be a place where anything at all could be uttered. And I wanted to get myself somewhere where words could be loosed. Truth, messy and free-flowing, would be allowed and even invited. I imagined useless social proprieties and platitudes left at the door alongside dripping umbrellas and false smiles. But I was a good girl, compliant, anything but a rebel. So when I was ready to fall apart I was careful to ask permission first. Is this a good time, Dad? Can I let go now?

There had to be something wrong with me. Nothing else could explain my misery, the sensation of choking. The family faces fixed so vacantly on my ferocious pain and fear led me to question my sanity rather than their honesty or impairment. It had to be madness, I reasoned, this sense of mine that our house was a haunted house.

Maybe I sought whatever I had hungered for at eight when I had wanted to be in an iron lung. I had seen a little girl in one in an old Danny Kaye movie. Her illness had brought both her parents running. I asked Dad afterward how you catch polio. "Well, Honey, I'm happy to report that thanks to Dr. Salk we've just about eradicated polio. You can't catch it anymore, so you can cross that off your worry list."

Maybe I sought the help I thought Jess had gotten. Mommy had gone to the hospital. Maybe I thought I would find her if I went to one. Perhaps it was Dad I thought I would find there. I knew that doctoring was what he did best, and if I went to a hospital maybe he would sit on my bed and hold my hand and know just what to do for the pain. He was confident as a doctor in a way he wasn't as a father.

Both of my parents had preferred hospitals to being home. Their respective hungers had been fed there, perhaps mine would be too. I might find whatever they had gone off in search of. Maybe I sought the calm pace and hushed tones I had discovered as a child while Dad made his rounds.

It was sanctuary I sought, true asylum. I wanted to pull in, to hide, to heal. I wanted to keep fresh pain from washing over me. I wanted to stop the flood of all that adolescence was bringing with it and to deal with what had happened so far. I wanted to step out of the rushing stream and to rest awhile on its bank.

Boys were trying to seduce my classmates, but something stronger sought to seduce me. The weight of guilt and despair and longing eventually would overcome me. But I was still years from surrender.

XV.

WHILE I WAS IN HIGH SCHOOL DAD LEFT HIS MEDICAL practice to study to become a psychoanalyst. The family problems likely inspired his decision and fueled his sincere desire to understand, to study, to become trained in handling such things. His approach was enthusiastic and scholarly. He could memorize a page of text in a wink and debate theory all evening. But all of his intellectual gifts seemed insufficient against the desperation ballooning under our roof and within the hearts of his four children. He and Barbara, awash in psychoanalytic theory, spoke in a new lingo now that seemed to puff them up and delight them, and distanced them even further from us and our pain. Whenever we talked, Dad's insights unfurled and the useless words droned on in the distance as I daydreamed of someone's arms around me and truth in my ear.

I was in 11th grade when Jess turned twenty, the purported end of adolescence, and days later he made his second serious suicide attempt. In time he was moved from the hospital in his college town to one in Manhattan, and he would live in the city, in the shadow of that very hospital, for the rest of his life. My own overdose would come at the same age. Nick at twenty would be in the Air Force. When Toby turned twenty, he would jump on his bicycle and spend the summer pedaling fiercely from New York to Oregon and back again. He would stop at payphones all along the way to call Dad and demand some answers. A determination to dispel years-old silences, to secure answers for himself, would propel Toby all the way from ocean to ocean.

As our teen years came to an end, so much remained undone and unanswered for each of my brothers and me. There were dangers swelling at our door and we had neither the tools to fight them nor safe harbor in which to ride them out. Adulthood loomed and we knew we were woefully unprepared. We were two or three steps back, stuck at an earlier lesson, trying to make sense of our childhood, of the silence and seeming disinterest at home. We had been trained not in self-discipline or self-reliance, but in other things. We were practiced in self reproach, in self pity and backward glances.

I deferred college after high school, not knowing what or where I wanted to study. I moved into New York City after graduation at Barbara's urging and got job in a small office. It wouldn't be a settled period, I would move eight times in nineteen months through a succession of rented rooms. But I hoped that in a city with so many options and programs and universities I would figure out my next step.

The greatest appeal to me of New York was the theater. I had been taking the train into the city and heading to the theater district throughout high school. There was nowhere I wanted to be more than seated in a darkened theater. On Broadway or Off-, musical or drama, concert or play. And movies served equally well. What I was after was escape to another world.

XVI.

I WENT TO WORK EACH DAY AND BEGAN ACTING CLASSES IN the evening. I performed small roles in school productions. Home again then to my typewriter, my ice cream, my TV, my self-loathing. Jess was out of the hospital and taking classes up at Columbia a hundred blocks uptown. He too was acting with a theater group and playing his music.

It is perhaps not surprising that acting and music drew both Jess and me. Performing provided an opportunity to utter the unspeakable, to externalize and unburden ourselves. It made use of the pain. It called it forth, it afforded a place for it and bestowed, at long last, permission to express it.

Onstage, we were heard. The audience attended in ways they did not in simple conversation or late-night phone calls. They even dressed up for the occasion, and sat in neat rows facing us. They tuned in, they listened, they hung on our words so that we would not have to.

Music was Jess's preferred means of expression. That was his wailing, his way of getting it out of himself, his flare sent out to the world. Maybe it would signal a helper. Maybe someone would hear the pain and come.

It was also an opportunity to give voice to someone who normally might not be heard, someone otherwise lost to the world. That was another lure of acting and music for Jess and me—we had always shared a heart for the dispossessed, the disenfranchised, to those voices shouted down and drowned out by louder, more sure ones. Mommy's was such a voice. And we wanted her to be heard. We wanted to hear her ourselves, to allow her to have her say at last. It fell to us, her children, to express her pain along with our own.

I studied my roles in earnest. There was escape in becoming someone else, relief at being handed a role, assigned feelings and words and motivations, raw materials with which to construct an identity, a character. Offstage I sought just such intangibles against the inner void. In acting, uncertainty and false starts were an accepted part of the process. And I wasn't expected to know my part too soon. It was understood that it takes time to create and compose a character.

Outside the classroom I went about my daily tasks acutely aware of how poorly I was performing as an adult on her own in the city. It was a role for which I knew I was

woefully miscast. I never knew my lines and panicked during those blank stretches. In real life no one stood in the
wings to whisper me through the unscripted silences. There
were friends, and I had a voice teacher with whom I talked
things over. But I dragged through my days feeling like a
fraud, knowing I was not fully in character, not well
grounded in the role I had been assigned to portray for the
rest of my life.

XVII.

I BEGAN TO HATE THE NOISE AND CHAOS OF THE CITY, AND I pulled in against it. Solitude became preferable to being with people. I was confused and hurt by my sporadic contact with Dad and Barbara, encounters by turns warm and chillingly detached. As I had in childhood with my mother, I took full credit for the switch but could never account for the changeability of their demeanor toward me. They seemed so easily to have cast me off. For years they had seemed almost eager to do so, to be done with my pain, to pass me along to someone else's care. Each meal together or phone conversation left me filled with a vague sense of self-reproach and longing for forgiveness.

Jess too was struggling. To stay in school, to keep his job, to stay out of the hospital. We both attended to the bare minimum of what needed to be done at school or at the office before we would hurry home to our respective caves, back into hiding. I gave the cashier the requisite few words—fewer yet as time went on—as I paid for the food with which I consoled myself in the evenings. I looked up and ahead as infrequently as I could manage.

Unsettled and anxious as my twentieth birthday approached, I quit my job. A new school year stretched out invitingly, but I did not know where to apply or where I belonged. The anniversary of Mommy's death came just five days after my birthday. A grayness settled over me as it always did this time of year. I planned to look for a new job but did not. I spent more and more of each day in bed, always tired.

I wanted Dad's hand to hold as I stepped into my twenties. I wanted Mommy, wherever she was. I wanted to be with her. I wanted to be with her or I wanted to be her, I couldn't remember which. But it didn't matter which one. Either way, dying was the requisite next move.

None of this was clear to me then, or calculated. I only knew I wanted to sleep and just after my birthday I filled a prescription for sleeping pills. I escaped the noisy city for a weekend at my friend Kay's house, and it was at there on Friday night that I took the overdose.

The idea had been with me all summer, and all week I had toyed with the vial. As I got into bed that night I took a pill and then, immediately, another. And then another. And then all of them. I reached for my notebook and began to write. The words, even and earnest at first, began to grow larger and wilder on the trip across the page as the pace quickened and the mind thickened. I was frantic to get it all said.

And then, instead of lying down I got up. I made my way to the kitchen. And I told Kay what I had done. Perhaps twelve minutes had passed. Perhaps twenty steps had brought me from bed to kitchen, from imitation to renunciation. Perhaps twenty years had brought me to this ambivalent, apologetic, angry reach for a life of my own.

Carry Back the Words

Give us the airways of the world, we dead,
but once on some still night when there shall be
no other sound and ether waves are free
to carry back the words we left unsaid.
We sleeping ones within each grassy bed
are restless with their weight and the decree
of endless silence. Give us then the key
that will unlock our prison doors — then, led
on unlimitable, starry space,
the crowded lanes will yield us each a wave
to reach some waiting heart, to say the things
it ached to hear. Ah, let us but retrace
our way upon the air, for then the grave
will hold the peace that such fulfillment brings.

—Nöel Gordon

I.

I WOKE TWO DAYS LATER IN THE HOSPITAL, THE SAME hospital Dad used to escape to when our home life overwhelmed him. I woke in that quiet, white place I had so loved as a child. It was the place where I had been born.

I woke up crying. A nurse told me where I was and what had happened, and I slept again. Sometime later I woke again and was told again. On Monday evening when I woke, a doctor was by my bed. And he was the one who told me about Stony Lodge, a small psychiatric hospital nearby. He suggested I go there and I agreed. I made the move that night.

In recent days, as the time to write about Stony has approached, I have found myself phoning or writing some of the people who worked there long ago. I wanted to hear them again, the familiar voices that had talked me through my time at Stony Lodge. I wanted to hear them and I wanted them to hear me. I wanted them to be thinking of me, to remember how it had been. I wanted them to go back in memory to that time and place so that I, writing and alone at my desk, would not be traveling back unaccompanied.

I called Laura White yesterday. She still lives in the same apartment near the hospital and still works there part time, though she's in Records now, no longer an aide on the Unit. She needs to work sitting down she tells me, her knees are no good. But it's clear that time has done nothing to diminish her good heart. And she is as ready to laugh as ever. It is decades since I first entered Stony's front gate and we met.

Mrs. Erdlitz is in her nineties now and still living in Florida where she and her husband retired more than thirty years ago. Every few months we touch base by phone or email. She was the formidable head nurse at Stony for years, though not on duty the night I arrived. She worked the day shift, she ruled the roost from seven to three.

It was dark when I arrived, and the admitting doctor was waiting for me in the main building. He wore an overcoat and kept it on during our brief talk. It was a cool autumn night. I answered what he asked and signed what he gave me to sign. When he called for her, the evening nurse, Mrs. MacDonald, came to the door—light hair, a gentle voice, a small smile. I followed her across a flagstone walkway to a white cottage, North Lodge.

Unlocking the door, she led me through a sitting room and down the hallway to a bedroom. Curtains at the window, a wooden headboard on the bed, the room looked nothing like a hospital. I was still dopey from the pills and Mrs. MacDonald reached out a steadying hand as I put on my nightgown. She wished me good-night as I got into bed and without thinking, I kissed her on the cheek forgetting where I was for a moment. I thought she was a housemother of some kind. I thought I was home.

II.

I SLEPT ANOTHER DAY OR TWO, BUT AFTER THAT I WAS REQUIRED to be up and out of my room each morning like everyone else. Soon after the day shift came on at seven, an aide would be in the doorway of my room. "Mrs. Erdlitz wants you out of bed." I hated the noise and brightness of the dayroom and left my room with reluctance and usually with tears.

I cried all the time. Barely across the hospital threshold and my mourning was begun at last. I cried so much that another patient cornered me one day and told me I reminded her of a baby, crying all the time. "When are you going to grow up and get angry?" she demanded and I slunk away, ashamed.

As I came to be more attuned to life on the Unit, it seemed in some ways that I had awakened in just the sort of heaven I had sometimes imagined for myself. At any hour of the day or night companionship was available. Mealtimes were unvarying. Things happened by the book and by the clock. It was clean and life was orderly. The locked door made me feel not trapped but safe. It gave me the relieved sense that nothing could get to me until I was ready to meet it. The staff members who held the keys were vigilant and alert to danger, so I no longer needed to be. I had been relieved of my duties. Other eyes had taken over the night watch and I could rest at long last.

But surrender followed surrender, and I lost my way for a time. A long period of confusion and struggle was begun, one I would not make sense of for years. I was at the age when it was natural to detach from my mother as a part of entering adulthood. But I had been left hungry by Mommy, we all had. There had been so little in the nine years that I had known her and the seven I had lived with her. And in those years she had held us so tightly, and had clutched us with such desperation, that any move I made away from her made me feel guilty and fearful.

Fidelity seemed to require that I suffer alongside her forever. Being happy or even alive was disloyal, and certainly selfish. And yet something in me was tugging to forsake her, to leave her to her choice, to decisively turn myself toward life, a life of my own. And so I added unfaithfulness to my long list of imagined crimes.

In small ways and then larger, I punished myself.

Something I didn't understand was playing itself out in my heart and on my body. It seemed that pain would pay a debt. But whose debt was I trying to pay with those wounds? My debt to her? Hers to the world? For whom was I suffering?

And even if I was unwilling to live out her life any longer, it was all I knew. I couldn't imagine what it would look like to live as just me, and I was afraid to find out. Afraid, afraid, afraid, in every direction. I was captive to fear. I was afraid of adulthood, afraid to be discharged, afraid to be set spinning on my solitary course.

I burrowed in at Stony, that clean, closed place. I curled myself around Mommy one last time and held on for dear life. She had chosen to leave us, her four children, but I would stage a final protest. I would refuse to accept her choice as I had refused all my life. I would not let her go.

III.

THE UNIT WAS THE PLACE OF COMFORT AND CARE. WITH the TV at one end of the dayroom and the nurses' station at the end opposite, the people I most wanted to be with appeared from behind the glass of one or the other. I apportioned my affection and attention between the inhabitants of the two. The nurses and aides were the ones who were there when I woke in the morning and if I woke in the night and during all the hours in between.

A group was gathered after breakfast each morning and taken down to the arts building for crafts and conversation, a change of scene. Soon after my arrival my name was added to the list and Mrs. Erdlitz strode over and urged me to go along, to get off the Unit. "You don't want to, I understand that. Do it anyway. Get out of that chair. I'm on my way to Staff Meeting and I want to be able to report that you're making an effort. But you've got to do your part.

Show them you're willing. Get up. Stand up. Have you showered this morning? Go get cleaned up. Join the party."

She was that combination that so fascinated me—firm command alongside compassion. There was no drama about Mrs. Erdlitz, no games or false flattery. She said what she meant and no more, and so what she said carried much weight. So I had to take her at her word then when she told me she had seen many kids like me get well. I valued her confidence in my future, but it also frightened me. I could not bear the thought of living again on the outside. I did not want to leave the hospital. And I was more ashamed of that secret than of anything else. I worried about what it suggested of my character that I was content to be there, that I aspired to nothing more than to live quietly in a locked cottage.

I met regularly with Mrs. Harrison, the social worker. Week after week we talked and we often seemed to be working at cross purposes, which we were. I wanted to know her, to charm her, to win her over. She wanted me on my feet and out the door. I sought retreat from the world, she demanded engagement. I wanted her to know my heart, she wanted me to show some guts.

I watched Mrs. Harrison and the doctors and nurses. I sought out glimpses of their private lives, although there were limits to what I wanted to see. I did not want the whole story, only those scenes that would confirm my imaginings. I did not want to see them bewildered, or floundering at home before a towering teenager, or cheating at cards, or barking at a waitress. I did not want to know if their marriages were cold or their hearts racist. I could not afford to sense them helpless or hopeless or mean. I did not want to see them drinking too freely. And I particularly did not want to see them shrugging their shoulders, fresh out of answers. I averted my eyes if I had to, if ever the truth threatened what I so carefully had constructed to feed a hungry spirit.

IV.

THE AIDES WERE BIG SISTERS OF SORTS FROM THE SOUTH and from Venezuela, Chile, Ireland, India, Mexico. They were lively and teasing and as different from one another as they could be. But each one uniquely filled a spot on the Unit that was theirs alone. We noticed and missed them when it was their day off. Bea was very quiet and very kind. I admired Ann's calm. Luisa had the best giggle. Marie was tough, but hilarious. Her husband worked at Sing Sing prison nearby and she brought us his work tales. Pat. Beryl. Cookie. Molly. They took us and our myriad anxieties far less seriously than we or the doctors did, so theirs was often the word we most needed. They brought in cupcakes for patients birthdays, pictures from a family wedding, a new board game. Becky brought songbooks one night, and we sang oldies all evening from the '30s and '40s.

Mrs. MacDonald came onto the Unit each day at three, and I always welcomed the sight of her. She was the first woman I met at Stony and would be the last to see me out the door. In between lay many hours in her patient, gentle company. At eleven she was relieved by Mrs. Bell, who worked all night. I often stayed up far too late to sit with Ma Bell. I liked hearing tales of life at her house with six kids, Dad and Grandma. I looked forward to our late-night talks in low light and low voices.

Who were these women to me? They were hope. They were possibility. I studied them as I sought to uncover or recover myself. I watched them come to work day after day despite family crises, bad weather, personal challenges. I saw them handling things, setting emotion aside, carrying on. In so much that they unknowingly exemplified, they helped to carry me a great distance and to set me on adult feet.

Even after she retired and moved away, Mrs. Erdlitz wrote me occasional letters telling me all the reasons why she knew I would make it. Her confidence in my basic sanity and strength fascinated me, and I wanted so much to merit it. "You have weathered so many problems and had the guts to keep going," she wrote, "You have so many qualities and strengths you are not really aware of," and I tucked her words away.

I hoarded encouragement and compliments, anything I took to be expressions of hope about myself and a future.

I stored it all up. In a spiral notebook I recorded every hopeful word I heard. Once they were set down on paper I would read and reread them, grateful for something solid to hang onto.

Sometimes I borrowed from the strengthening of others. There was an evening when Nancy, a new patient, left out a card that her mother had sent, and I read its brief message. "Hang on, my child. Joy comes in the morning." I thought I had never read anything so lovely. I even copied the promise into my notebook and whispered it to myself for months and years afterward. I used to pretend that the message was personal and intended for me by a loved one. It would be a decade before I discovered the treasure of Psalm 30 and realized that was exactly what it had been all along.

Weeping may go on all night, but joy comes in the morning.

V.

IT WAS DIFFICULT AT TIMES TO TALK BUT UNLESS THINGS were very bad I could write and I wrote nearly every day, sometimes all day. I filled notebook after notebook, several thousand pages before it ended. I wrote down what I could not bear to hear spoken, what I did not trust anyone with. I wrote to give it a form outside myself so I could set it down and walk away from it. I wrote to make it real. I wrote to save it up for later, like Dad and his home movies.

Writing helped to save me somehow. A corner of my brain detached and dedicated itself to recording and commenting on the proceedings. It seemed to know that I would need an anchor thrown out to keep me from drifting too far. Writing was the foot I kept planted on the ground when hopelessness and darkness threatened to carry me away. It was a healthy impulse that kept me scribbling. It was the trail of crumbs I cast behind me to lead me back when I returned. Writing was a wedge I used to keep a door from slamming and locking me out.

My notebooks recorded in grim detail my struggle with life, with being alive, my wrestling with abandonments behind me and adulthood just ahead. But many as there were, the writings did not tell it all. There were no words for some of it and I could not write at the worst of times. There were long periods when I never left my corner at the sound of the bell, and those days went unrecorded. I chronicled some of the falling, some of the flight and fight. It was there in part, but not the fearsome whole of it.

It is tempting to try to present in clear, down-to-earth terms what happened. It is appealing from so many years' distance to try to rationalize those months of my life, to try to put an amusing spin on it all. The urge is to tie it up neatly, to tell my tale without the sloppy edges, without all the mess that spilled over the sides of the pan. I would like to skip right over much of it, to offer up sense in place of the nonsensical.

My life-saving sense of the ridiculous inclines toward making comical the embarrassing or inexplicable. My rational, analytic mind wants to plot a clear course in reverse to show how Z quite naturally and understandably resulted from Y and X, and to trace it even further back to Q and to P before that, all the way back to C and then B and finally to A, the source. But I cannot explain all that went on. I only know that there was a long moment in my life when I dwelt at Z. And I know it because old journals from the back of a closet tell me so. And they tell me in my own handwriting. And they tell me that Z was an untidy and horrible place to be.

My doctor predicted that in time I would grow up and grow stronger and that the darkness would lift for me and my thinking would straighten out. And he was right. But for all his credentials and the staff's professional training, for all the treatment plans devised with such care, in the end what led me down the hill and out the front gate were patience and compassion. I had been afforded kind escort as I toured the turrets and ledges of a broken heart and spirit. I had been accepted and encouraged by those who saw me at my most unlovely and unlovable—the very definition of home.

VI.

WHEN THINGS WERE AT THEIR WORST AT STONY, MRS. MacDonald used to tell me that someday I would come back for a visit with a husband at my side and a baby in my arms. I didn't believe it but I loved her for believing it. And I liked hearing the tales and details of a future she and the others envisioned for me.

Some years later I did go back to visit. I did not yet have a baby in my arms, but I was happily settled in a wonderful marriage and about to start graduate school. It was Mrs. MacDonald herself who saw me at the door and, grinning, unlocked it to let me in. We sat a few minutes in the dayroom and she teased me about being an old married lady. We laughed and caught up. I mentioned in passing an Austria trip I had made two years before, and she surprised me by saying, "you always talked about taking that trip."

Had I? I didn't remember. But she did. She and others remembered long-standing dreams of mine and they kept them for me. And there were other dreams they claimed for me before I knew enough to have them.

We had enough to talk about that day of the present and future and did not venture into the past. The sole reference to it was made as I was leaving. We were standing at the door of North Lodge and the key already was in her hand, the key that would allow me to leave that place for the last time. "When did you let go of your mother, Laura?" she asked me. "That has freed you."

During that same period and for years afterward, Barbara and I continued to have to work at making sense of one another. It came neither naturally nor easily. But by the end there was peace. I was alone with her in the middle of one night when she was dying. It was years after Dad's death, and she had had a massive stroke. She was moaning and trying to move about on her mattress, unable to say what she needed or where she hurt. And it threw me back with such force to those terrible nights in Austin that I was as terrified and helpless as I had been as a child of eight or nine with my mother. I sobbed as I wiped Barbara's face and removed her nightgown to replace it with a cooler, clean one.

And that's when I saw it—her soft tummy, her breasts, a freckle on one shoulder. I stood a moment, unmoving. Underneath, she looked just like me. In thirty-five years I had never known it, had never suspected the tender hidden self. All that time and it was only armor that had been scaring me off, the sharpness and chill of armor. Beneath it was a woman, a girl, a heart as eager to be known and heard as Mommy was, as I was, as we all are. I wish I had known it sooner. But I knew it now. And I dressed her and I kissed her and I asked her forgiveness, and I gave her mine.

In the years just after Stony, Dad and I had begun at last to thoroughly enjoy our shared temperament and sense of humor and many interests. We swapped books, we spent long evenings in conversation and playing word games. On my twenty-first birthday he had baffled me with the gift of a typewriter and thesaurus. Long before I did, he knew I would write. It was just as my twenties were ending that Dad was diagnosed with cancer. And the end came so quickly that almost before we could believe he was ill, death had come and he was gone.

VII.

THE DAY OF DAD'S FUNERAL WAS THE LAST TIME THE BOYS and I were together. Jess would die four years later. All four of us took part in the service with readings or reminiscences. I was crying hard throughout the service and as I anticipated the moment I would have to stand up to give the eulogy I had prepared, I despaired. "I don't think I can do it. I don't think I can do it," I kept whispering to my husband at my side. Squeezing my hand for courage he reminded me how much I wanted to pay this tribute. "If you don't do it you will regret it deeply," he told me, and I knew he was right. The hard thing was the necessary thing.

Dad had belonged to a community chorus and the group lined up now to sing "Jésu, Joy of Man's Desiring." And as the music began I watched none other than Mr. Dunn step in front of the chorus and raise his arms.

Nothing could have been more moving to me or fortifying at that moment than the sight of Mr. Dunn conducting that magnificent music. His fluid arm movements and those eloquent hand gestures calmed me as they had years before when Jess and I were in his high school chorus. In the moment when I needed it, God orchestrated the most comforting image possible and, minutes later, it allowed me to stand up and do one of the hardest things I had ever done.

In high school Mr. Dunn used to call out to us as we sang, "Listen to what you're saying. Listen to the words!" The words! They have been in my heart ever since. "Blessed are they that mourn, for they shall be comforted." "He that rules over man must be just." "How lovely is Thy dwelling place." "My Redeemer lives." "And His loving kindnesses are forever unto those who fear Him." Years before I knew Him, God was daily feeding me on His truth and hope.

Months after Dad's funeral I opened the Bible at a friend's urging. And reading a handful of ordinary words something in me woke up. *He himself bore our sins in his body on the tree.* I saw *sins* at the center and felt a new conviction, but also something like relief. Finally a voice willing to affirm the truth I long had known. How much had it cost over the years for me to gain the uneasy victory against the urge to punish or even kill myself for things I had not done or caused? I had narrowly won against false guilt. And yet, and yet, my heart always had whispered, what of true guilt? What of the wrong you have done, thought, spoken? And here, in a word, I saw it. Had I not known all along that payment was due?

And yet the verse said my sins had been taken. Christ had taken them into His own body on the cross. My debt to a holy God had been paid in full. Christ on the cross says to me *It is finished.*

That day for the first time I saw myself for who I truly am and I saw Christ for who He truly is. A sinner met her Savior. Years before, I had accepted the vital truth that my mother's death was not about me. Now I came to the far greater truth that Christ's death was about me. And the verse continued, *By his wounds you are healed.*

VIII.

J ESS LIVED IN THE SAME APARTMENT IN THE BRONX FOR
twenty years. After I left Stony we always seemed to meet
at a coffee shop or museum. Somewhere along the way he
had stopped inviting me to his place. He stopped inviting
anyone. By the time he died, none of us had been in his
apartment for almost a decade. His world had grown very
small by then, and contact with him was limited and sporadic and always on his terms.

After his funeral and the burial in Texas, Toby and I
planned to meet at Jess's apartment for several days of packing and cleaning up. Going into that apartment was something we had thought about for years. I had long imagined
a visit with Jess there, making a meal together as he told me
about his latest great find at the Gotham Book Mart. Or
playing our guitars in his living room surrounded on all
sides by those tall bookcases and his beloved books.

We knew Jess lived in chaos, and I liked to think of

setting his world to rights, of washing clothes or bedclothes in warm sudsy water and hanging them to dry in fresh air. Toby had also been waiting gently but urgently for Jess to let him in. For years he had been armed with grocery sacks and his peaceful, easy demeanor waiting for the door to open a crack. Toby had stood by with his powerful urge toward life and his wholly uncritical spirit, ready and eager to scrub or simmer or polish. He carried with him all the ingredients for one of his consoling vegetable pies. He had the batter mixed and ready for a plateful of hotcakes.

We would have done it all, anything we could have, anything Jess would have allowed us to do. In those day-dreams of ours, Jess opened his door to us. In those day-dreams we stepped through his doorway and into his arms, not through a "crime scene" tape and into dead silence.

When the police tape was gone, and we were free at last to enter, I found that I could not. I could not bear to smell or to taste the air in that closed apartment where Jess had died. I could not bear the quiet of his absent guitar stolen from the apartment in the days just after his death. I could not bear to witness the squalor in which he had lived. I was unwilling to store those images in my mind's eye, more than unwilling. My memory already was crowded to overflowing with images and scents and sensations I fought to suppress.

Toby could not have been more compassionate or generous with me, and he went to the apartment alone. He was compelled by something that I understood deeply and completely. He kissed his wife and son good-bye and he went to New York to let air and light into those rooms. He went to shovel and throw out and sponge off and realign and restore. He forced himself to dwell for days and nights where Jess had lived and died. Toby did it all and he did it all alone. It was among the bravest things he has done in a life that has often called for bravery.

IX.

THREE YEARS AFTER JESS DIED I TUCKED THE SEVERAL volumes of his journals into a bag and flew alone to the Arizona desert. I went to a town where I knew no one. I went to a place near no other place, a room with no distinction or distractions. I took a taxi from the airport so I had no car, no means of escape. I went at the height of summer when the July sun was burning hot and clean. I stayed indoors and I read years of Jess's life.

I made myself read it through, read it all. I forced myself to hear it and to know it at last. Jess had shared himself in the only way he had been able, and I would listen. I would serve him as witness. I would read the detailed accounts of things he had lived through as a child and adolescent, things I had never known.

I learned that I had meant something to him. I read on page 41 that he loved me. Pages later I found myself on a "To Do" list. I was item #16. He was going to get in touch with me after he had done fifteen other things. He had worried about me one day in 1979. He sketched my smile in another volume on page 88. In February he thought something I had done was sweet. I was still at Stony on page 132 and he feared he was losing me, that I was going to die.

I had opened Jess's journals seeking to affirm the experiences of his solitary life, but I found as I read that he was doing as much for me. In page after page he described the childhood that I myself remembered, the mother, the father, the days and nights we had passed together and apart. He confirmed my memories, even those I had felt disloyal thinking about and had begun to doubt. But here it was set out in Jess's black and white—my childhood emergent from someone else's pen.

In one entry written years before he died, Jess wrote, *"Where can I get enough sleeping pills to die? I need maybe fifty of them. It'll hurt my brothers and my sister so much, but I'm sorry. I'm terribly sorry that I can't make it, my brothers, my sister. I am destined. No. I'm not. I choose to do it. I want to die. Not because I am destined, but because right now my memories and the intense job of relating is too much. You can't imagine. It's incredibly tough to exist, to try and make it. You can't believe all the pain."*

But I could believe it. When Jess wrote that entry, I was still at Stony months after my own overdose.

How was it that Mommy's death left us with such an appetite for death? For years Jess and I passed a death wish between us like teammates with a ball, like forwards moving downfield toward a common goal. He never saw the suicide note I had written that night at Kay's, but much of it he could have dictated himself:

"Just took all the sleeping pills. Waiting. Finally some peace. I tried to be good and act alright but it's too hard. There's so much more to say."

X.

THERE WAS SO MUCH MORE TO SAY. AND THE URGENCY I felt to speak it, to convey in words all that was yet unspoken, ultimately meant life for me. Years afterward I found the big box filled with my hospital notebooks when I was looking for something else in an office closet. Opening one at random, I was shaken by the record I found there, embarrassed by the girl I had been in my twenties. I tore up handfuls of pages and threw them away and stashed the unread remainder back in the box.

Months later I was drawn again to the box, and again began to read. But this time I read the volumes through. I read them with different eyes and with the beginnings of compassion. I spent days revisiting a period of life that I did not entirely remember, one I did not want to remember. But the same determination that had propelled me through Jess's writings now drove me into my own. I would rejoin the lost loved one and I would listen.

For months at Stony I had dwelt without full allegiance to either death or life, committed to nothing and no one. The only authorities to which I had yielded had been my own longings and fears, and they had ruled me. Lacking a weighted core to bring me back to center, I had been tossed and blown by every urge and emotion. The writings told a story but not a neat one, not an even tale. There was no clear line to carry a reader from beginning to end. Rather those entries formed a jagged series of steps—two up, six down, and then another down before beginning up again. The result was an erratic and rambling stairway that seemed throughout to have no landing.

At the time I came across the journals I had not thought of this period in years. And yet it was so immediate and as I read I remembered so well, too well, the pain of it. I was yanked back with unanticipated force. It was achingly fresh—the inability in those days to express, to even understand, what I was wrestling with or to convey it to anyone. It seemed to be the moment in my life for this. I could not have read them any sooner. Twenty years had passed—exactly the length of my life when I had arrived at Stony.

How painful and frightening life was then. It was challenging to read through the notebooks. I had to walk around and around our neighborhood with my husband each evening and cry a while in the cool air. In the mornings I would be up before six and out the door again to run and run, alone this time.

I was soothed by those talks, by the tears, by time. I knew by now that Mommy was a person wholly separate from me. That truth had come as a double-edged sword, but accepting it had changed things. I knew now too that her death was separate from her love for me. Her choice did not reflect the depth of love she felt for anyone. *But if she had really loved me she could not have done it.* But she really did love me and she did do it. The two are not related. They are separated by the distorted thinking and excruciating pain of a suicidal depression. Her death was the choice she made. And it was an act for which she had to take responsibility. Finally I did not.

XI.

I FOUND MARCELLA IN 1997. IN THE END IT TOOK A SEARCH company only ten days to find someone I had wanted to find for close to thirty years.

She had come to live with us the week Mommy died and I had liked her immediately with her red hair and brisk manner. She had cooked and cleaned up the boys and me, and had taken command of the chaos at home. And late at night I would sneak into her room to pour out my heart in whispers as later I would do with Mrs. Bell.

She was my haven in that year after Mommy death but in the years since then she had grown larger in my mind and heart. When things weren't right or I needed answers or direction, my thoughts often turned to her. *Marcella would know what to do. If only I could find Marcella.*

My search over the years had been an informal and sporadic one. Visiting a new town I would sometimes call people in the local phonebook who shared her last name, but it was not an uncommon one. I had little else to go on. In 1997 I heard about a search company that was reuniting adopted children with their birth parents and I hired them for $144. Just ten days later an envelope arrived in the mail while I was away for the weekend at a women's conference. When I got home on Sunday, there it was—a single sheet of paper containing her address and telephone number. She lived in Maryland, in the county where I recently had lived for five years. She lived in the town where I had worked.

Should I call? It was already 9:30 at night there. She would be in her 70s by now. Was it too late? I had to call, I had waited so long. I dialed and almost held my breath until a woman answered.

"May I speak to Marcella, please?"

A pause. "Who's calling?"

I gave my name and explained in brief.

"This is Marcella's daughter. I'm here packing up. My mother died two days ago."

Two days. Would the pain have been less sharp if I had learned she had died years before? Probably. The timing, however, was God's, although it would be a very long, angry time before I would be willing to consider His hand or purpose in any of it. But later I could not help but consider the timing of finding my friend on that particular

Sunday evening in light of the conference theme of that very weekend—Hosea 10:12 *It is time to seek the Lord.*

Nearly a century ago Oswald Chambers wrote, "Our soul's personal history with God is often an account of the death of our heroes." How many deaths has God used to turn me to Himself? How many deaths and how many lives? How many examples of endurance and selflessness and mercy have surrounded me. How many moments in my life of correction, of restoration, of hope, point to Him who alone could work such grace.

XII.

WHEN JESS DIED, HE LEFT MUSIC BEHIND. AMONG MORE than one thousand albums and tapes and CDs in his apartment were recordings of his own performances—concerts and multi-track recordings of practice sessions with Jess playing four different instruments and singing three-part harmony with himself. He had recorded one song more than a dozen times, an old bluegrass tune, "Will You Miss Me When I'm Gone?" Over and over in different keys, at different speeds he sang it. And over and over for almost twenty years we have lived out our reply. And it is yes.

Anger came quickly when Jess died, even as I mourned him. Within a day or two of the news the anger came. It felt wrong but it felt right. After Mommy died it would be fifteen years before I stopped blaming and punishing myself. Fifteen years of pity and excuses for her and recrimination for me. Fifteen years unwilling to say to her No! This is wrong! This you cannot do.

Suicide does not end pain, it transfers the pain to others. It multiplies and compounds it. It breathes new life into it so that the pain gathers force and spreads out and lasts and lasts.

I have been tempted by suicide. I arrived at Stony at twenty mesmerized by what death seemed to promise—escape from pain, and all the comfort and sweetness of having a mother. Death was where Mommy was and so death was where I thought I wanted to be. I had grown up feeding on a little couplet of hers, one of her many renderings of death's promise—

Death is burning, gentle light.
Free of shadow, death is white.

She had written it when she herself was twenty and a boy she liked had drowned, the brother of a high school friend. His death led her into the same dangerous, romantic false thinking that her death would for me.

But something happened to me in the early days at Stony. A thought came to mind, a question seemingly out of nowhere: "What if you're wrong?" What if death is not as you have always imagined? What if it is not the absence of pain after all but rather something dark and unending? What if *There* is worse than *Here?* I had my fears about living, but this new notion of death was even more fearsome. And it caused me for the first time to regard death a stranger and to step back from it, uncertain and afraid. In that instant the possibility of suicide was removed from me, and I felt it as the loss of a friend.

It would be a turning point, one of many, when I realized that death was not necessarily whatever I imagined or wanted it to be. Death might be sweet and it might be hell, I did not know. But whatever it was, it was. My thinking did not determine it. My wishes could not alter it. Not I but someone else had determined the way of it. Not mine but other hands had drawn its dimensions. It was not mine to say what death was, or when or how it would come.

XIII.

NICK WAS OUT OF TOUCH FOR MANY YEARS AFTER JESS died. The silence was painful, but I understood it. What we had in common was pain, and contact easily veered into misunderstanding and hurt feelings. We had not spoken in ten years when I saw Nick in a dream one night. I was entering a little chapel just as he was leaving it to step into the surrounding cemetery. As we saw one another he stepped toward me and opened his arms, shaking his head with obvious regret. We embraced in silence and stood holding one another for a long time. "It's alright, it's alright," I wanted to say. "I understand the silence."

He called me days later. His voice was hoarse and I didn't recognize it at first. But we talked easily then for several minutes, updating one another on our families and lives. And then came the reason for both his call and his hoarseness, he had cancer. And as he started the detailed play-by-play of the preceding two weeks of tests and results, I remembered the almost identical conversation I had had with Dad sixteen years before, almost to the day.

Dad lived a few weeks after his call. Nick lived almost three years. He died at 51. During those three years Toby and Nick and I spent days in Nick's home and in his hospital room talking, laughing, delighting in one another. During long months in the hospital we marveled at how unfailingly patient and upbeat Nick was with the nurses and staff almost continuously in and out of his room. There were frequent flashes of Dad's humor and talent for mimicry. While a blood transfusion was being hooked up he would admonish the nurse, "check the type! That's not from a country music fan, is it?"

Nick's guitar, his prized Martin, was always within reach, even in the hospital. He sometimes played during our visits. We talked about the years we had been apart. We talked of the days and nights at Doe Hill, and Nick's memories confirmed my own, as Jess's had. We spoke of Mommy and Dad with compassion and gratitude and without the anger of our youth. So many hard things in us had softened in the years since losing our parents and in the years since becoming parents ourselves.

As winter was ending, Nick died. Both Toby and I spoke briefly at his funeral. There was so much more I would like to have said about who Nick was and about the victory that his adult life represented. But the size of the crowd that filled the chapel that day spoke its own word about his life and influence and overcoming.

I remember a dream Toby once had. He was perhaps in his thirties. Like my dream of Nick, his had no words. Toby, tall and grown, was vomiting sand. Simply that. He was vomiting and vomiting sand. At an aquarium recently I was stopped short by the exhibit label on a tank full of sand dollars. I stood there nodding my head as I read, remembering Toby's dream.

"Where waters are rough, sand dollars hold their ground by lying flat or burrowing under. Adults also fight the currents by growing heavier skeletons. Youngsters swallow heavy sand grains, which weigh them down."

XIV.

I AM BRIEFLY IN NEW YORK AND GO OUT TO THE DOE HILL house on a clear October afternoon. However many times I have driven past this house over the years I have never seen a sign of occupancy, never anyone in the yard or on the porch. Today, though, the place is crawling with life. Workers in white painters pants and caps and t-shirts are everywhere perched on ladders, scaffolding, hanging out windows, at every level, on every face of this house.

The front shrubbery is shrouded in white drop cloths but the house is white no longer, and the porch no longer blue. Years of paint are gone. The entire house has been scraped and soaked and stripped down to bare wood. Porch and house are uniform now, the color of honey. Here and there not only is paint gone but the siding itself is missing. Rotted lumber has been cut away in places and tufts of insulation peek out of the holes. They look like sore spots but with a good chance now to heal, exposed as they are to the sun.

In every direction is motion, exertion, as surfaces are sanded and smoothed. I can almost smell fresh lumber. I can almost hear a large, sun-baked house sigh with relief unbound and freed of faded color and the grime of decades. Even the picket fence is gone now, one less encumbrance. With window shutters stacked against a tree, the house looks wide-eyed and alert. On a bright afternoon I have caught that gorgeous moment between past and future.

As I drive by I do not pull into the driveway to turn around as I have always done before. Instead I continue past the house and up the hill beyond it. Have I ever driven up here before? At the top of the hill I turn into the first side street I come to and pull off the road to park. I have just seen the house as I want to remember it forever. I sit in stillness realizing I will not come here again.

Not ready to leave, I get out of the car and start to walk through woods in the direction of the house. A *No Trespassing* sign nailed to a tree warns me against this trek. Leaves are thick underfoot as I make my way around large boulders. I have a vague memory of the boys and me climbing this hill on a spring day when yellow flowers were blooming and we couldn't wake Mommy from the couch.

Just beyond another *No Trespassing* sign is the brow of the hill, and the house is there below me—the back door and kitchen window frame are clean and exposed. Painters in white work here too, squeezed into the narrow shadowed passage between house and hill.

My mother often stood at the sink looking out that window. Her daily gaze met this hill thick with trees, rough with rock, pressing up against the house. Behind her four voices called out for feeding, for comfort, for rescue, for answers.

In your honor I breathe deeply, Mommy, as you could not. I wish you could have stepped out of that house to climb this hill. I wish you could have stood where I stand now. There is wind here and a far view. I would like you to be standing at my side, our feet on firm ground, your beloved hand in mine.

Long ago you unfolded the heart of your daughter and left it open and hungry. That was the last you knew of me, your last guilt-ridden glimpse. But my heart is full now, and I want you to know it. It is filled with music and loved ones and the peace of God. My heart is His resting place and His heart is mine. I am yours but I am His, and I am home.

If the LORD had not been my help,
my soul would soon have lived in the land of silence.

—Psalm 94:17

ACKNOWLEDGMENTS

No laboring woman has been surrounded by a more sustaining and patient circle of midwives than I have been. This work had its beginning many years ago, and from the start I was encouraged and steered by Mary Nilsen, Sharon Billings, Kathi George and Ursula Michelson. I have been unfailingly cheered up and cheered on by Clara Kennedy, Sharon Meins, Youlika Masry, and my friends at CBS. My agent, Ellen Stiefler of Transmedia, carried me along by her enthusiasm and efforts, and to Barbara Bachman of Random House, who did layout and design, my most heartfelt thanks for so beautifully dressing this precious baby of mine.

My son patiently shared his childhood and his mother with this most insistent sibling. My husband has offered constant encouragement, invaluable critique and perspective, and unfailing love. I would not and could not have completed this without either of you.

PHOTO: © JENNIFER GEORGE

LAURA GORDON GEORGAKAKOS is an editor and writer who has collaborated on books for Harcourt Brace, Sierra Club, Zondervan, DK Publishing, HarperCollins West and others. She is the co-author of *Wild Discovery* for Discovery Channel and *Billy Graham: God's Ambassador* for Time-Life Books, and is a popular retreat and conference speaker. She received her B.A. (Phi Beta Kappa) in American Literature and M.A. in American Studies and is a graduate of the New York Academy of Theatrical Arts. She and her husband, Kosta, have been married since 1984 and have a grown son. They live in Southern California.